STO

OVERSIZE

S0-DRH-927

3-9-76

The Railroad Saga of Jeff Keenan

From trainboy to engineer, "Jeff" Keenan's life has spanned the history of the great railroads, and it reaches its climax in his establishment of Narhfam—the National Railroad Hall of Fame and Museum. Profusely illustrated with rare, historic photos of famous old trains and trainmen, *Railroad Saga* is bound to become a collector's item. Today "Jeff" Keenan, whose work reaches across the United States from New York to Oregon, lives in Portland, Oregon, busy with his railroad projects and his writings.

Jeff Keenan writes: My odyssey into railroadiana began when I first observed the movements of New York Central and Hudson River "shunter" number 74 at Black Rock, New York, a hamlet later annexed by Buffalo. Fired with adventures from tales of Frank Sawyer (gate tender at the Dearborn Street crossing, opposite to Black Rock station) and being of a restless nature with an inquiring mind, I wanted to go places and see things.

In a day before the general use of the automobile—when radio and TV were unheard of—living in a community could be singularly provincial. But there was one aspect of Black Rock which spelled romance, far-off places, and the great beyond. That was the arrival and departure of passenger trains.

Selling newspapers on standing trains at Black Rock station during custom inspection prepared me as a trainboy at the age of 11. Employed as a brakeman at the age of 13 started my unprecedented railroad career—first as the youngest brakeman, and at the age of 15 the youngest fireman, and at 17 the youngest locomotive engineer in the history of Class 1 railroads in the United States.

During the years that followed I served various railroads in different capacities and also attended the University of Chicago for special studies. Eventually I settled down and married a wonderful woman, as of October 16, 1915.

The rule, years ago, was not to employ a person for train and engine service who was under twenty-one years of age. Nevertheless, many boys lied about their age to get on railroads and I was probably the biggest liar of all. Most of those boys were imbued with that pioneer spirit to help themselves regardless of the amount of work connected with the job. Most of them felt, as I did, that it was a privilege to work for a railroad. My adventurous spirit took me from the Coal & Coke Railway in 1906 to work-train service on the Deepwater Railway, building east to meet The Tidewater Railway building west, to form The Virginian Railway.

From the time I was a trainboy, my avocation has included plans for construction of a permanent home for enshrinement of our great railroad and locomotive builders and persons memorable in railroad history. During the past several years, token exhibits have been made in various cities. Certain cities, especially Ogden, Utah, are in hope of becoming the permanent home of the National Railroad Hall of Fame and Museum.

Cover Photograph

Southern Pacific Lines Locomotive No. 4449 was loaned to the American Bicentennial Commission to pull a 24-car "Freedom Train" through various states as part of U. S. Centennial activities, thereby becoming one of the famous steam locomotives in modern railroad history. (see page 44) Photo courtesy Kennell-Ellis Studio.

THE
RAILROAD SAGA OF JEFF KEENAN

by

C. J. "Jeff" Keenan

Binford & Mort

Thomas Binford, Publisher

2536 S.E. Eleventh • Portland, Oregon 97202

Loyal Order of the Caboose

To all lovers of switch engines, vista domes, train callers, engineers' bandannas, and conductor watch chains ...

know ye that _____ C. J. Keenan _____

by virtue of his deep understanding of the services rendered by railroads and for his loyal support above and beyond the call of the train whistle, is hereby declared and will henceforth be designated a member in good standing of THE LOYAL ORDER OF THE CABOOSE.

Membership herein entitles the holder to all the various rights, privileges, recognitions and considerations rightfully due to those who believe that railroads are and will remain a vital part of the economy and security of the United States.

SIGNED

Harold J. Turner – Chief Cabooser

S. H. Mallicoat – Recording Cabooser

Ken Rinke – Validating Cabooser

DUES _Loyalty and Friendship_

R.R.

The Railroad Saga of Jeff Keenan

Copyright under international
Pan-American copyright conventions
Copyright © 1975 by C. J. (Jeff) Keenan
All rights reserved including the right
to reproduce this book, or any portions
thereof, in any form except for the
inclusion of brief quotations in a review.

Library of Congress Catalog Card Number: 74-24496
ISBN: 0-8323-0248-1

Printed in the United States of America

First Edition

Jeff checks the time of his 50-year-old-watch in hope that NARHFAM will arrive at greater stations on time in our American Heritage.

As a member of the "Loyal Order of the Caboose" in good standing and my dues, "Loyalty and Friendship" prepaid, and my seniority dating back to the time that my attention began to focus on hearing the puffing of locomotives and an occasional whistle nearby, I now have prepared an autobiography of my life, mostly of my railroad career, for publication. The composition is the result of encouragement by eminent people who know of my past activities, especially during the years I have been dedicated to the National Railroad Hall of Fame and Museum, part of our American Heritage.

Railroading is fast changing its complexion. Many factors are contributory to the changes. With such transitions, it becomes more demanding that there be preserved evidence of the heritage that this country and its people have in the railroads. To those who—through direct involvement, association, and remembrance—have been close to railroading through the years, there is strong interest in preserving this heritage. For the current generation and generations to come, there is need to make available the fascination and significance of railroading past, present and future. NARHFAM is dedicated to accomplish this purpose through a planned building that will be a monument to the immortals enshrined therein.

DEDICATION

To Helen White Keenan, my beloved wife.

CONTENTS

PART ONE   JEFF KEENAN'S STORY 9

The Early Years 9

Trainboy 10

First Years as a Brakeman 18

Locomotive Fireman and Engineer 29

Brakeman - Conductor - Motorman 30

Return to Civilian Life 34

NARHFAM - The National Railroad

     Hall of Fame and Museum 37

National Railway Historical Society 38

Honors 41

Meeting Other Eminent Persons 42

Enshrinements - Hall of Fame 46

Enshrinements - Hall of Romance 62

Thomas Alva Edison 66

The Brave Engineer 71

PART TWO   RAILWAY PHILATELY 72

PART THREE   GALLERY OF TRAINS AND LOCOMOTIVES 90

American Locomotives 90

Canadian Pacific Lines Locomotives 139

Acknowledgments 147

Index 149

Left: C. J. (Jeff) Keenan as a brakeman for the Coal & Coke Railway at the age of thirteen. Right: His father.

Coal & Coke Railway passenger locomotive No. 18 in service between Charleston and Elkins, West Va.

Coal & Coke Railway freight locomotive No. 55 in service between Charleston and Elkins, West Va.

PART ONE

JEFF KEENAN'S STORY

THE EARLY YEARS

Most unusual. . .teen-age parents. . .Father's mete-oric rise in the newspaper world. . .Mother becomes a notable actress. . ."farmed out" to my mother's cousin—"Aunt Mary" to me. . .my father's rise in business and art. . .my mother the "anthracite brunette". . .President McKinley. . .Aunt Mary con-ferred the name of Keenan upon me at time of bap-tism. . .my father appointed minister to Denmark.

I was born in Toledo, Ohio, January 14, 1892. Although my railroad career was unique, it can be said also that my early life was most unusual. My parents were only eighteen years of age, having married in 1891. They both aspired to become eminent in their respective fields of endeavor; and they distinguished themselves in a few years, my father as a newspaper publisher and editor and my mother as a notable actress.

However, my father's meteoric rise in the newspaper world and my mother's desire to re-main on the stage gave very little time for family life. I was soon "farmed out" to my mother's cousin, who resided in Buffalo, New York. It was she who gave me the love I needed to enable me to enjoy a normal life. My parents' careers kept widening the marital gulf between them that eventually resulted in an uncontested separation. Nevertheless, they both kept in communication with Aunt Mary and me until their death.

Father served as cashier and later as business manager for the *Detroit Tribune*, 1892-95. He was secretary and manager and later editor and publisher for the *Chicago Daily Journal*, 1895-1905. As of October 31, 1905, the *Daily Journal* was merged with the *Chicago Daily News*. At that time he returned to Detroit as editor and publisher of the *Detroit Tribune*. Within two years he became president of Booth News-

papers, Inc., which included newspapers published in Grand Rapids, Flint, Saginaw, Kalamazoo, Jackson, Bay City, Muskegon, and Ann Arbor.

His "Horatio Alger" career empowered him to become a director of four of the leading banks of Detroit, namely, Guardian-Detroit Bank, Detroit Security Trust Co., Union Joint Stock Land Bank, and Selective Securities Corpora-tion. He was vice president of the Associated Press, 1917-18. He served as president of the Detroit Institute of Art and the City Art Com-mission. He promoted the handsome new building for the city's Institute of Arts, which opened in 1927. To the new museum he pre-sented many gifts which included old and new masterpieces from Van Dyck to Degas. Some of the paintings which he particularly prized—the ones that later went to Washington—he hung on the red damask wall of his drawing room.

Father was also a director of the Detroit Symphony and vice chairman of the Detroit Chapter of Red Cross. He was appointed United States Minister to Denmark, January 22, 1930, but died while serving this office in the Ameri-can Legation, Copenhagen, Denmark, June 20, 1931.

Mother continued to excel in repertoire under her maiden name, Rachel Richards for stage publicity. She was born in the province of Que-bec, Canada. Her father was of French lineage and her mother a Keenan, born in North Caro-lina. She was known on and off the stage as an "anthracite brunette." Her hair, coal black, added to her great beauty. I called her cousin "Aunt Mary," who must have had a lot of pa-tience with me because I grew up to be an ad-venturous and spirited lad, headstrong at times.

I remember my first year as a pupil in School 20 in Buffalo, where I got along better with the girls than with the boys. My teachers helped me to get ahead because I wanted to learn, thus enabling me to skip the fourth grade. I well recall my teacher for the sixth grade—a striking brunette whom I adored. After school I sold newspapers at Black Rock Railway Station, just a short distance from Aunt Mary's home.

I was in charge of the station newsstand on the day that President McKinley was shot by Leon Czolgosz in the Music Hall of the Pan American Exposition. I sold hundreds of extras. Black Rock Station was only two miles from where the tragedy occurred. Newspapers were in such demand that most conductors held up the departure of their trains until I had passed through all cars. The President died eight days later, on September 14, 1901.

Although I concentrated upon the job at hand, I couldn't help hearing the puffing of locomotives and an occasional whistle nearby. So, at that time a longing was established that carried me to a notable career in railroading. I made friends with train crews, which led to my taking short trips on trains until I was threatened with expulsion from school if I continued playing hooky. Later the station master informed me that I could take charge of the newsstand regularly—which added to my income from the sale of newspapers.

I had to be at the station before 6 a.m. to be on hand to sell newspapers to workmen riding belt-line trains of the New York Central & Hudson River. These trains ran six days a week carrying workmen that regularly filled five and six cars. The runs circled the city of Buffalo and suburbs, stopping at the more important streets that crossed the railroad or were adjacent thereto. These runs started again soon after 5 p.m., and many of the people who rode these trains would depend upon me for their newspapers. The sale of newspapers at the station did not interfere with my school hours, during which time the station master took over. Homework was generally given to pupils who did not make much progress during classes. I made it a point to seldom have home studies.

New York Central & Hudson River "shunter" 74—that switched cars in Black Rock yards—was my favorite locomotive during my early school days. Many times on weekends I would ride it, sitting on the fireman's seat box. In those days of the link and pin, yard crews worked seven days a week and twelve hours each day as a rule. The fireman allowed me to shovel coal into the short firebox and I would brag about it to my friends, but I didn't mention it to Aunt Mary for fear that she would put a stop to it. The crew taught me some of the rules of "safety

first" which left an imprint on me that most likely saved me from serious injury in later years.

I asked one of the switchmen why they always referred to locomotives as "she." He said, "You be around the station at noontime and you will see the reason." I was there when a Canadian Pacific passenger train stopped for custom inspection after crossing the International Bridge over the Niagara River from Bridgeburg (now Fort Erie) to Black Rock. The switchman had finished his lunch and came alongside the well-polished locomotive. After the train departed, he asked, "Did you notice how careful the engineer looked her over as though she was his pride and joy?" He also remarked, "Some engineers are known to love their locomotive more than their wife. Now you should know why locomotives are referred to as SHE."

TRAINBOY

Picked from kindergarten as a trainboy. . ."Fat Pickens," supervisor at Zanesville, Ohio. . .wild ride on the "rods" to win a bet. . .each day was education . . .allotments from my father purchased artifacts for our American Heritage. . .learning Morse Code at age of twelve. . ."O S ing" trains by at Charleston Depot. . .adventures of a trainboy on the old Coal and Coke Railway. . .meeting United States Senator Stephen Benton Elkins, also vice president of the Coal and Coke Railway.

It was during the spring of 1903 that a supervisory agent of the Union News Company called on the station master at Black Rock to inquire if he knew of any young men who would be interested in serving as trainboys ("news butchers"). The station master replied that he knew of a boy who could fill the job, if the boy wanted it. The agent asked where he could contact the boy and was told that he was standing behind him. When he turned to look, his first remark was, "I am not picking them from the kindergarten." The station master replied that he was confident I could handle the work.

Before the day was over I was employed, after securing permission from Aunt Mary. She was reluctant to give in, but then as she said, "I don't want to check his ambition to succeed."

New York Central & Hudson River Railroad switcher No. 74. It was later sold to the Newark & Marion Railroad as No. 3, about the time the Pennsylvania Railroad took over the electric line.

Kanawha & Michigan passenger locomotive No. 577, and (below) switcher No. 561 at Charleston, West Va., depot.

Mullens, West Va., 1906 (top), and 1956 (bottom), former terminal of The Virginian Railway.

I was given a uniform cap, badge, and brass buttons to fix to my blue suit and then instructed as to what trains to ride to Zanesville, Ohio. Before my departure a few days later, Aunt Mary and I sat down and had a real cry that I shall always remember. It was to take a long time for me to get over the loneliness caused by being away from her. Whenever it was possible I would return to be with her even if it was for only a day. I felt she was my guardian angel. She always remained a bachelor woman.

Whenever my mother played in Buffalo, she would always stay with her cousin—Aunt Mary to me. It seemed like a homecoming for her and an event for us. We would always see her off on the train leaving the old Exchange Street Station at Buffalo, and there were real tears in our eyes each time she boarded the train for other cities of the circuit.

During the years after leaving Aunt Mary I would visit with my mother if we happened to be in the same city. At her performances she always arranged for me to have a good seat. After the curtain went down following the last act, I did not have to be a "stage-door Johnnie" to be with her. I would go back stage and wait until she was dressed for the street. We would then always go to a good restaurant and eat and talk.

I also remember how men would endeavor to meet her. Flowers and other gifts were conspicuous in her dressing room. However, I am confident that she never stopped loving my father, which had much to do with her never marrying again nor going steady with any other man. Once when she was given quite an ovation, she threw a kiss to me that had people in the audience stretching their necks to see who the lucky guy was.

At Zanesville I worked under the supervision of a roly-poly man whose right name was Tom Pickens, better known as "Fat" Pickens. I followed his instructions and he helped me to increase my commission, which was 20 per cent of the sales. My first trip was on a Baltimore & Ohio train bound for Chicago. The first time I passed through the cars with a basket full of fruits, salted peanuts, and candies, I tried to sell some of the wares to people seated in the dining car waiting to be served with food. After returning through the diner from the Pullman cars in the rear, the steward followed me into the vestibule and in a fatherly way informed me that it was against the rules for the "news butcher" to give "competition" to the service in a dining car.

I then made friends with the steward—which paid off. When his patrons would ask where they could buy certain things that only I had to sell, he would direct them to the head car where my merchandise was spread out for sale. The steward resided in Chicago and when I picked up my Chicago newspapers at Chicago Junction (now Willard) I would always give him a copy. At Chicago I would visit book stores to purchase textbooks and other publications pertaining to railroads. I gained a good measure of education from textbooks, and for a change read railroad books that I would sell later on trains at a profit.

At Zanesville I would visit the trainmen's room—off by itself in the station—and listen to trainmen and enginemen "shoot the breeze." One evening a conductor told about a hobo who was removed from the rods of a recent passenger train arrival by the big redheaded Irishman who was employed as a railroad policeman for the Zanesville area. The conductor further said that the hobo put up a fight in which he got the worst of it and was then marched off to the jail a few blocks from the station—which meant that he would be put to work cleaning the streets for a few days. At the time it appeared to me that the officer was also the judge and jury.

As I listened in on the conversation, I blurted out that I could ride the rods without getting caught by a "cinder dick," which was the term applied on certain occasions during those days. (Later I learned to have a lot of respect for railroad police officers as most of them were family men and quite decent if you respected the law that they are employed to enforce.) A switchman spoke up and wagered five dollars that I couldn't ride the rods to Newark and return without being caught. I readily accepted the challenge. It seems that the redheaded policeman heard about my taking the dare. He warned me if he caught me riding the rods he would take me to jail and put me to work cleaning the streets.

One dark evening I waited in my overalls and jacket away from the station platform, and when the conductor called "all aboard!" I crawled upon the wooden slats fastened to the iron rods that reinforced the undercarriage of wooden cars at that time. When the train started to move I was relieved. En route, a heavy rain came down and at each road crossing the mud and water splashed on me. When I finally crawled out from under the car at Newark, the first person I approached was the night sergeant of the Newark police force. Until I spoke to him, he had not recognized me all covered with mud. Then he burst out laughing, saying, "What kind of a circus stunt are you pulling off?"

When he composed himself, he added, "What made you do such a foolhardy trick?" He then said, "Follow me but don't get too close." When we reached the jail near the depot, he handed me a bar of yellow laundry soap and what could pass for a towel, directing me to a rain barrel behind the jail. Then he said, "Wash yourself even if you have to stand inside the barrel; also wash your clothes. I will try to find some clothes you can wear until yours dry on the radiator. When you are through there will be some hot coffee you will need after the time you will spend out here in the cold." He fixed up one of the cell beds for me to sleep on. I must have needed rest and sleep after my escapade.

I slept until morning, then dressed in my overalls and jacket, which were dry by that time. The cell door was open. I stepped across the street to the restaurant where the smell of food soon made me forget my adventure of the night before. Luckily, I still had some money that I started out with to pay for the hearty meal I ate. The counter waitress recognized me and asked, "What are you doing in overalls?" About that time a police officer whom I knew and who had heard about me remarked, "I hope that you learned your lesson playing the role of a hobo." When the waitress questioned me, I told her about my foolhardy trip.

A train was due soon for Zanesville. When I boarded it, Conductor Howard had to be told about the caper—which produced a hearty laugh on his part. He was a robust man and when he laughed his belly rocked up and down. He remarked, "I guess the men will insist that you join them in shooting the breeze one of the coming evenings." When I related my experience to the group, the switchman who made the bet with me said, "You owe me $2.50 because you rode the cushions on the return trip." He agreed to the flip of a coin to see whether he or I would pay the $2.50. I won so he paid me.

Trainboys were changed on runs when their sales fell off to some extent, and that happened to me. Subsequently I learned that if I was to keep my job, I had to give more attention to selling merchandise than to the girls who rode the trains. After a lecture that was in order, "Fat" Pickens placed me on a run of the Cincinnati & Muskingum Valley, now part of the Penn Central, between Zanesville and Washington Court House. At the latter point there was a layover of one hour before returning to Zanesville. This run provided for every night in Zanesville.

At Zanesville I was also introduced to the Ohio River & Western, a narrow gauge railroad that operated between Bellaire and Zanesville from August 28, 1902 to Memorial Day, 1931. This railroad was nicknamed "Old Rusty and Wobbly" by the rural wits of the Monroe County hills. Passenger trains terminated at the Baltimore & Ohio depot at Zanesville. Prior to August 28, 1902, it operated under the name of Bellaire, Zanesville & Cincinnati, and was nicknamed "The Bent, Zigzag & Crooked."

As the opportunity came to me, I signed up for a run on the Cleveland & Marietta Railway between Cambridge and Marietta, Ohio. I had to "dead-head" between Zanesville and Cambridge with my merchandise each day while on the run. During the summer months, there were weekend excursions between Marietta and Cleveland, Ohio, leaving Saturday evening and returning from Cleveland on Sunday evening. These trips were profitable. Couples, especially, would eat a lot of sweets and spoon until they fell asleep. Always there were passengers on return trips who were hard to awaken at their destination, remaining on the train until it reached Marietta. They would then have to pay the fare back to their home town—and also have to wait until departure of the regular train. The C. & M. later became a part of the Penn Central.

When Tom Pickens was transferred to Columbus, Ohio, in 1904, I went with him. During the first few weeks I worked from the extra board. My first regular run was on night trains between Columbus and Dunkirk, Indiana, over the Pennsylvania Railroad. The sales were low on regular merchandise. I had to resort to selling contraband items such as ham sandwiches that were purchased in the Columbus Union Depot restaurant at five cents each and sold for ten cents each, a 100 per cent

Top: "FIDO" — purchased for the Deepwater Railway on March 13, 1903. Product of Altoona, Pa., shops, litter of April 1873. Deepwater Railway No. 30 (center) and Tidewater Railway No. 13 (bottom). Both railroads became components of The Virginian Railway.

15

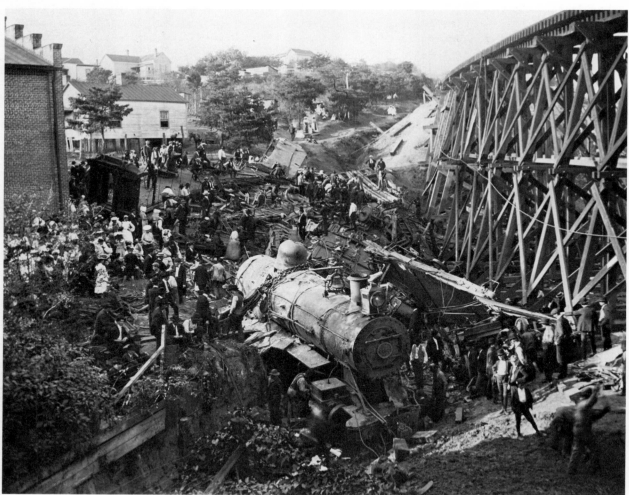

Top: Southern Railway locomotive No. 1102 lying on side in "The Wreck of Old 97," and (bottom) being raised for placing on tracks for taking to repair shop.

profit. I wrapped them in paper napkins to keep them fresh. Seldom were any left over and I went hungry until the return trip arrived at Columbus. I could have doubled my profits with the serving of hot coffee along with the sandwiches, but of course there was no way to keep the coffee hot.

Regardless of what my commissions were, I always tried to keep my expenses within the amount of my profits. Whatever other income I enjoyed was generally put into a savings account. My father would send allotments to me at intervals. However, throughout the years that money has been spent for the purchase of artifacts and other items pertaining to railroads for our American heritage.

As time passed, I became eligible for a day run between Columbus and Charleston, West Virginia, over the Toledo & Ohio Central and Kanawha & Michigan railroads. These two railroads were closely allied and well operated with only a change in locomotives at Corning, Ohio. I found my layover in Charleston to be interesting, but the evenings long until it became known to me that I could help the night agent during his twelve-hour shift at the depot. For my help he taught me the Morse Code in a few weeks. Then I was taught to send Western Union telegrams, and later to receive messages. The depot was the only place in the city to send and receive messages.

I was also soon trained to properly set the semaphore boards which indicated to engine and train crews the movement of trains. The semaphore pole had two boards, one on each side for signalling trains in opposite directions. This was known during those days as the manual block system. Some railroads still use that system. If there were no train in the block ahead I would set the semaphore inclined downward; in addition, at night a green light would be displayed. If there were a train in the block ahead, I would set the board at a half angle and display a yellow light at night. If there were train orders issued by the train dispatcher that the engineer and/or conductor would have to sign for, I would set the board in a horizontal position; in addition, at night a red light would be displayed. Another part of my training included the "O S" of trains by the station. The O S was a report transmitted to the train dispatcher and to telegraphers at the advance and rearward stations; for example, train Number 77, locomotive Number 362 or extra

locomotive Number 359 had cleared Charleston depot at 8:45 p.m.

One evening as I was "O S ing" a train by, I made a slight error in transmitting that the train dispatcher detected. I was a little panicky at the time and turned to the night agent for help. It was then that the train dispatcher learned for sure that someone was helping out during the busy period. However, he must have thought I would fit in as an operator on the night trick at Dickinson—which was soon to be available—until he was informed that I was only twelve years old.

I well remember one evening on which I was about to "O S" a train by. It came to a grinding stop that had the flagman hanging onto the hand-hold from the rear platform of the caboose—to keep from being thrown to the rails below—and the conductor charging through the door of the caboose cursing with each step. When the conductor returned to the depot, he rendered a report to the train dispatcher about setting out two cars damaged by the crushing stop of the train. The part that created a sensation along the line and in offices was as follows: "My engineer slowed down to about 15 miles per hour upon observing a yellow board and light. Coming out of a fog bank about 1200 feet from the depot around a curve at that point he saw what appeared to be two red lights on a caboose only a few feet ahead. He stopped the train as quick as possible. Suggest that the superintendent handle with city officials to have the madams along Railroad Street change the color of the lights advertising their business from red to green in order to avert repetition of such accidents as what happened to this train tonight."

The Kanawha Valley was noted at that time for fog banks that would settle for short periods over the railroad in places. On that night one of those fog banks began to lift as the train rounded a curve adjacent to Railroad Street, with two red lights looming up ahead in the parlor window of one of the houses and showing up as two red markers on a caboose.

The Kanawha & West Virginia interchanged freight traffic with the Kanawha & Michigan at North Charleston. Like the K. & M. it later became part of the New York Central system. The K. & W. V. operated passenger trains into and out of the K. & M. depot at Charleston, which added to the duties of the night agent. I continued my evening work at the depot until I transferred my activities to the Coal & Coke

Railway, after discussing the matter with both of the agents at Charleston Depot. They informed me that my commissions would be greater than on the T&OC-K&M run.

As I adjusted myself to the new runs between Charleston and Elkins, West Virginia, my commissions increased, amounting to more than on the T&OC-K&M runs. The night layovers alternated between the two cities. The majority of passengers were miners, lumberjacks, drummers, and women. They were good spenders as long as their money held out. Paperback books were quite in demand, including such titles as: *Through Missouri on a Mule*, *Slow Train Through Arkansas*, *Opie Read in the Ozarks*, *Jesse James*, and other exciting stories. Some books sold were considered sex at that time but would be classified as moderate today.

One of my sales pitches was to pass through the coaches and give each passenger a small scoop of salted peanuts. (The trains were well filled in those days.) Later, when most passengers were hungry for more salted peanuts, I would pass through with a basket full of sacks of peanuts and make many sales, sometimes emptying the basket.

I recall some unusual incidents that happened during my services as a trainboy on the old Coal & Coke, now part of the Chessie System. Outstanding was the time a circuit-riding preacher boarded the train at Blue Creek with a live rattlesnake which was used during his sermons. It was common practice for these preachers to pass through the cars and talk to passengers about the Bible, or—in extreme cases—try to convert a person. Once when a preacher was talking to a miner's daughter, the snake found its way out of the box and took over the smoking car. Passengers dashed to the baggage car ahead and the ladies' car behind. When the preacher was informed of what was happening in the smoking car, he remarked, "Please do not disturb me during this service." A minute later a miner who had remained on the platform looking through the door window of the smoking car rushed in telling the preacher that the "newsbutch" had just put a bullet through the eyes of his snake. This angered the preacher into shouting, "The devil will get him for that." During the scramble I was able to "borrow" a rifle belonging to the express messenger by telling him that the smoking car was full of "rattlers." The rifle hung in plain view on the wall of the baggage car. Just before the train pulled into Gassaway where the preacher got off, he beckoned to me to sit down with him. He said that he was sorry for his early remarks and wished to assure me that I was a courageous lad.

My introduction to United States Senator Stephen Benton Elkins started one day at Clay Court House (later named Clay). As I stepped down from the train to sell newspapers to some of the townsmen, I noticed a distinguished gentleman speak to Conductor Tom McConihay and then board the train. I asked Tom about the man and was told that he was also Vice President of the Coal & Coke Railway. He further remarked that the senator and his father-in-law, Senator Henry Gassaway Davis, were the builders of the railroad, and that they also owned all the coal for miles back from the railroad right-of-way. I learned later that the statement was not as farfetched as it sounded at first. I also learned that Mr. Elkins was born in Missouri but won fame as a United States Senator from West Virginia. His father, Kit Elkins, and the grandfather of past President Truman were close friends back in Missouri. The senator became one of my customers on the long trips between Clay Court House and Elkins. At that time most of the legal work for the railroad was conducted at Clay Court House and that was the reason for his frequent trips.

FIRST YEARS AS A BRAKEMAN

Senator Elkins instrumental for my employment as a brakeman on the Coal and Coke at the age of thirteen. . .adventurous spirit took me to The Deepwater Railway where I was hired as a brakeman at the age of fourteen. . .meeting Henry Huttleson Rogers on station platform at Page. . .also met Sally Morgan, the prettiest girl in that part of West Virginia, whom I would have married but her parents said the age of fourteen is too early, but would consider a marriage at the age of sixteen. . .meeting Elias Hatfield. . . memories of The Virginian Railway, notably the moonshiner who had his still and bar at the top of Matoaka Gap, where I tried my hand at poker playing instead of drinking "likker". . .Number 18 foamed and water went out the smoke stack—fear of a boiler explosion. . .wild and bloody times among the Slav laborers when "likker" was available.

FORM 880.
NEW FORM 790—STANDARD.

Chicago and Eastern Ill RAIL ROAD

Chicago DIVISION.

CERTIFICATE No. *903*

Impression copy to be taken in book
kept for that purpose.

OFFICE OF *Superintendent*

Jan 18th 1918

THIS IS TO CERTIFY, That *C. J. Keenan*
has been employed in the capacity of *Brakeman*
At *Danville* on the *Chicago* Division
of the *C & E I RR* Rail from *Dec. 6th 1911*
To *Jan 17th 1918*
Reasons for leaving service *Resigned*

Age *31*
Weight *170*
Height *5 ft 7 3/4 in*
Complexion *Light*
Hair *Light*
Eyes *grey*

J O Bell
Superintendent

SIGNATURE OF PARTY TO WHOM ISSUED: *Charles J. Keenan*

Left: Jeff in uniform as a passenger brakeman walking to the rear of train to afford flag
protection until all the mail and express was unloaded and loaded at Chicago Heights,
Illinois. Right: Jeff at 22. Bottom: His Service Record — Chicago & Eastern Illinois
Railroad—Date of employment - Age given as 24, correct age 19 years. Date of resignation
- Age shows 31, correct age 26 years.

FAMOUS HATFIELD CLAN

Front row — Tennis, son of Anne; Levica Hatfield, daughter of Jonse; Willis E., son of Anse; and Yellow Watch, the dog.

Second row — Mary Hatfield Simpkins (later Howes), daughter of Anse, and her daughter, Levica Simpkins, in her arms; Anderson "Devil Anse" Hatfield; Levica Chafin Hatfield, wife of Anse; Nancy Smith (Glenn) Hatfield, wife of "Cap" holding her son, Robert; Louise, daughter of Nancy and "Cap" standing between them, and William Anderson "Cap" Hatfield; the boy standing next to "Cap" and holding the pistol is Coleman A. Hatfield.

Back row — Rose Lee Hatfield; Troy Hatfield; Betty Hatfield; Elias Hatfield; Tom Chafin, relative of family; Joe Hatfield; "Ock" Dameron, hired hand; "Sheppie" Hatfield; girl at corner of house, Levica Hatfield; man standing apart from group at right, Bill Barden, store manager at Devon, Mingo County, at mouth of Beech Fork, friend of family, who made arrangements for the photograph, taken April 1896 in Logan County.

Virginian locomotive No. 202 at Page, West Va. Also shows picture of Elias Hatfield, between two trainmen in uniform, at the time he was employed as special agent for The Virginian Railroad and Ritter Lumber Company. Note the antlers on the headlight.

One day, in the smoking car, I remarked to Senator Elkins that I would like to become a brakeman. He smiled and said that I was quite young for that kind of work. I told him that, on several occasions, Engineer Ambrose Tierney had let me shovel coal into the firebox of Number 18, the locomotive that was regularly used on that passenger run, and that I could set brakes, couple and uncouple cars, and knew the hand and whistle signals. He then suggested that I speak to Superintendent Johnson.

A few weeks later I took advantage of the opportunity to speak to the superintendent after he finished talking to the senator on the station platform at Gassaway. Before the senator returned to the train, he said to the superintendent, "My young friend here thinks he would like to become a brakeman." Before I could put words together to ask for a job, Conductor Tom McConihay called all aboard and that meant me as well as the passengers. A few days later I was the first person to step off the train at Gassaway. I lost no time in crossing the station platform and climbing the stairs to Superintendent Johnson's office. I stood before the door, hesitating a few seconds. Then hope and determination carried me on. I knocked on the door and a voice from within that I recognized said, "Come in."

Again, words began to fail me. However, I finally got hold of myself and asked if I could go to work as a brakeman. He looked me over and then inquired about my age. I said twenty-one. He looked at me again with a half smile, knowing I had lied about my age, and said, "Son, you are going to be twenty-one for a long time. I am giving you a trial. Be sure and watch your step. I don't want you to get hurt on this railroad." My home terminal was Gassaway.

It can be said that the senator enabled me to obtain my first employment as a brakeman on Friday, October 13, 1905, at the age of thirteen. This started me on an unprecedented railroad career serving as the youngest brakeman; then at the age of fifteen the youngest locomotive fireman, and at seventeen the youngest locomotive engineer in the history of railroads in the United States. This was due in large measure to a great man, owner of railroads and vast bituminous coal property, who was not too big to help a very young man in his ambition to become a brakeman.

The rule, years ago, was not to employ a person for train and engine service who was under twenty-one years of age. Nevertheless, many boys lied about their age to get on railroads and I was probably the biggest liar of all. Most of those boys were imbued with that pioneer spirit to help themselves regardless of the amount of work connected with the job. Most of them felt, as I did, that it was a privilege to work for a railroad. My adventurous spirit took me from the Coal & Coke Railway in 1906 to work-train service on the Deepwater Railway, building east to meet The Tidewater Railway building west, to form The Virginian Railway.

I first met Henry Huttleston Rogers on the station platform at Page, West Virginia. I was wearing a derby hat, often referred to as a "diser" or "bowler." He remarked that I was the first trainman he had ever seen wearing a "diser." As our conversation continued, I was able to identify myself as the son of Ralph Harman Booth, whom Mr. Rogers asserted he had met in Chicago a few years before when my father was publisher and editor of the old *Chicago Daily Journal*. Perhaps if I had remained with The Virginian Railway I might have received steady promotion.

Henry Rogers' career is one of the most significant and fascinating in American business history. He was the man who, singlehanded, conceived and guided to completion The Virginian Railway, and he played an outstanding role in the development and growth of American industry and commerce. His attempts to interest other businessmen in the project were unsuccessful. As a result, he found himself virtually alone and unsupported in the scheme. In the face of serious obstacles, including the financially constricting Panic of 1907, he stubbornly pushed ahead. Finally, his dream materialized to an impressive reality—a railroad from interior West Virginia to the sea was opened in April of 1909. A financial success almost from its inception, The Virginian Railway proved the accuracy and perceptiveness of his vision.

Rogers later became a director of various railroads. He was involved in the Harriman railroad empire, serving as a director of the Union Pacific Railroad. The Virginian Railway, of course, was the capstone of his illustrious career. He died on May 19, 1909, but lived to see trains moving over the entire length of this important railroad. He was elected to the National Railroad Hall of Fame and enshrined as of July 4, 1960.

Allan Nevins, the historian, in his biography of Abram S. Hewitt—son-in-law of Peter Cooper and former mayor of New York City— tells of a visit made by Henry Rogers to Hewitt's home in 1902. On leaving, Rogers said to his host, "I have enjoyed myself so much that I would like to leave a little gift for the Cooper Union. I want it to be recorded as anonymous." He handed Hewitt an envelope. Fifteen minutes later when Hewitt thought to open it, he found a check for $250,000.

When Peter Cooper died, the City of New York went into mourning to pay tribute to a man who had been called "the first citizen of New York City." With very little education, he had managed to combine innate intelligence, personal drive, and a broad social consciousness in a productive career that was dedicated to the public good. His inventive genius was always at work. In 1829 he built the "Tom Thumb" for the Baltimore and Ohio Railroad, the first successful locomotive to be used in America. The word unique has often been used to describe the Cooper Union, which may explain why, unlike other educational establishments, Cooper Union is found in *Webster's Unabridged Dictionary* with the definition, "An institution in New York City for practical teaching for the working classes in applied science and art, founded by Peter Cooper in 1859."

Like Henry Rogers, Peter Cooper was elected to the National Railroad Hall of Fame and enshrined as of July 4, 1960. The Certificate of Award reposes in Cooper Union, Cooper Square, New York City.

Page was the main terminal for The Deepwater Railway during 1906-7. Locomotives were repaired in an oblong building, large enough to hold two locomotives. The Deepwater had the reputation of keeping their locomotives in good repair and clean. Two mixed trains, freight and passenger, operated between Page and Deepwater and between Page and Mullens. No tickets were sold for passage on work trains between Mullens and the supply yard at Matoaka Gap. All anybody needed was the conductor's permission to ride in the caboose.

While riding the mixed trains, my flirtations with girls were happy experiences; and girls haven't changed much during the 20th century except for clothes, hair-do and sophistication. Although there was at that time much less sensationalism and artificial amusement, I am quite sure that life for boys and girls was more harmonious. Most girls were pretty even in their inexpensive clothes. They were affectionate and they acted more natural than girls of later years. However, they also could play the role of bashfulness with finesse.

The prettiest girl in that part of West Virginia was an innkeeper's fourteen-year-old daughter, Sally Morgan. She was a brunette with lucid brown eyes and entrancing figure. Her pappy's hostelry was just a short distance from the cinder platform with a sign sticking up in the center designating West Deepwater. All Kanawha & Michigan trains operating between Charleston and Gauley Bridge stopped there. Most of the passengers who got off there were destined to points on the Deepwater Railway. A shanty was used by passengers jointly with the Chesapeake & Ohio Railway on the opposite side of the Kanawha River.

The innkeeper was also the ferryman of the rowboats for transportation across the river. If there were a few ripples on the river, that meant delay in crossing, sometimes till the next day, to the disgust of passengers—until they were served with good food by a very pretty girl.

A Deepwater brakeman—also fourteen years of age—sat with this pretty girl on the banks of the Kanawha many times talking about this and that until they heard the shrill of Uncle Billy's whistle. Like the mountaineers who stopped in their tracks to catch the last echo of the captivating chimes of Uncle Billy Richardson's whistle, we were deeply stirred when we heard the first shrill of his whistle as his train rounded Lovers Leap approaching Gauley Bridge. People on both sides of the Kanawha River rushed to their doors and windows to catch a glimpse of him and his long white beard at the cab window. To them Uncle Billy was a symbol of a great man at the throttle of a famous train, the Fast Flying Virginian. They all looked upon him with reverence, even the pretty girl sitting beside me. When Uncle Billy whistled passing the Deepwater depot I couldn't mistake an extra pressure from the hand clasped inside mine.

To get from (and to) the K&M side to the C&O shanty cost fifteen cents to pay the ferryman, who sometimes was me as an assistant to the innkeeper's daughter. People in the area informed me that Sally was a granddaughter of General John Hunt Morgan, known by them as "The Thunderbolt of the South."

Top: Big Four No. 373 — Chautauqua type. Bottom: Big Four No. 373 with plaque on boiler reading "Universal Exposition — Saint Louis — 1904."

Jeff Keenan

Helen White Keenan, wife

Mary Helen

Ann Margaret

Gertrude Elizabeth

Dorothy Theresa

Jeff Keenan with wife and daughters

Frequently I would ride down on the train from Page to Deepwater to be with Sally. The distance was about twenty miles each way. On one of these occasions as I was ferrying the rowboat, Sally and I discussed—as we had at other times—getting married. A couple who were steady passengers listened in on our plans and then told Sally's mother and dad. That same evening I was called into their parlor, where Sally was sitting in one corner with a dejected expression. Her father said to me, "We like you very much, but you and Sally are too young to marry. You wait a couple of years and if at that time you still feel that you want to marry and Sally feels the same way, we will give our permission and we will plan a real wedding for both of you."

We would not have discussed our plans for marriage at that time if the subject had not arisen about the refusal of the Justice of Peace at Amstead to take paper money sometimes because a few persons had paid him in confederate currency which the bank turned back to him. This led up to my plans to go to the bank at Montgomery fifteen miles west of Deepwater to exchange paper money for silver dollars.

Novel experiences were more the rule than the exception during my service as a brakeman for The Deepwater. Rattlesnakes were common around Harper, and everybody respected them. However, one day I stepped down from the locomotive without first looking. Surprise at the sight of two squirming snakes within striking distance (disturbed by escaping steam from the locomotive) landed me at the bottom of the grade, which made my position no less dangerous. There was some quick thinking on my part. I shouted to the fireman to shovel hot coals from the firebox and toss them down the grade to make a path for me to return to the tracks. It was a hotfoot experience, but free of snakes.

At Maben, I first met Elias Hatfield, son of Captain Anderson Hatfield, also known as "Devil Anse" and leader of his clan in the feud with the McCoys. Elias was employed as a special agent jointly by The Virginian Railway and Ritter Lumber Company to keep order in that area.

Self-protection was the strongest in the younger Hatfield sons—particularly Elias and Detroit, commonly called Troy by his mountain buddies. The word was widely spread that these sons were best left alone. But their reputation for being able to take care of themselves even-

tually brought them employment. When The Virginian Railway found it necessary to employ detectives to stop mountaineers from shooting at trains passing along Slab Fork between Mullens and Princeton, Elias and Troy got the job. After the Hatfields were placed on the payroll, the trouble along Slab Fork stopped. Elias and Troy left the railroad in 1910 and opened a saloon at Boomer, West Virginia. In a business agreement with a fellow saloon keeper, they divided the town and fixed the area in which each could sell. But their competitor afterward broke the pact by hiring an Italian to peddle liquor in Hatfield territory. When the brothers learned of this trickery, they went to the mountain shack occupied by the Italian to warn him away from his practices. Elias approached from the front, Troy from the rear. When Elias opened the front door, a bullet struck him in the heart. He had no gun in his hand at the moment he swung back the portal, but when he was picked up dead later, a revolver was clutched in his fingers. After shooting Elias, the Italian whirled and fatally wounded Troy, pushing in from the rear. But before this brother died he fired three shots. One bullet struck the Italian between the eyes, another in the heart, and the third in the bowels. Doctors said any one of the three would have been fatal.

Some weeks later I was called to "deadhead" (to ride on an authorized pass) to Mullens for work-train service between there and Matoaka Gap supply yard. It was several weeks before the regular brakeman returned. However, during that time there were stirring incidents. Ascending Matoaka Gap, cars were pushed ahead of the locomotive because of a dearth of switching facilities at the supply yard. I was the head brakeman who rode the first car as a lookout.

After the evening meal—which was served by a commissary operated by the Ritter Lumber Company—members of the crew, along with other employes, would stroll up the path leading to a moonshine bar near the top of the gap where "likker" was served. The man who ran the bar candidly told his railroad customers, "Revenooers will never stop us from making corn likker as long as people want to drink the stuff." The bartender said he had the right to make moonshine likker, that it was a family operation handed down from father to son. He perpetuated tradition in his woodshed, never lacking for company once the sun dipped behind the hills. The building exterior was built of mine timbers and boards. The interior was resplendent with mirrors and brasswork comparable to what you would ordinarily see in bars of some cities.

When The Deepwater men came into the area, the bar took a turn for the better or worse. The grading gang arrived first to kindle a spirit of merrymaking for each evening. Weeks would pass and then the bridge force would spend many evenings at the moonshine bar before going on to the next camp. Again weeks would pass before train crews, track layers, and other employes would arrive and stay awhile before breaking up their abodes for the next point of operation.

During these periods some patrons of the moonshine bar were characters who left their imprint of hilarity, like Tom Galway, the Irish locomotive engineer assigned to Norfolk & Western Number 18, which was rented by The Deepwater for work train service. After swigging down a few drinks of moonshine likker, they had forgotten they were miles from civilization and cared less. There was no other way to spend earnings, unless they were permitted a few days off for a trip to Bluestone, where they could be entertained by "wine, women and song," a distinction not all of the townsfolk there were enthusiastic about but one they put up with back in 1906.

To get to Bluestone from the Gap, one had to walk ten miles—unless there was a track tricycle going to Matoaka—and then pay to ride a Norfolk & Western passenger train. For some, this was an obstacle to making the trip. That gave the moonshine bar of Matoaka Gap a corner on recreation as it was. The Irish locomotive engineer came to sing and recite poetry, and a track-laying foreman to drink and relieve tensions of the day. The commissary clerk brooded over the desire to be with a woman, constantly contriving ways and means to get to Bluestone. A conductor of Falstaffian stature attended sessions at the bar to show off his talent for imitations of stage personalities and the telling of wild tales. Poker players operated in the barroom without fear of being tricked by professional gamblers.

It was this barroom that I visited occasionally for a poker hand. I let moonshine alone. I saw what it did to others. I never understood how grown men willingly drank to stultify them-

selves, only to revert to smartly disciplined workers on the job the next day.

In ascending Matoaka Gap, Tom Galway, the engineer, would try to straighten out some of the curves, as the saying goes among railroaders. The stakes to retain the loaded rails on flat cars would creak and rend the air as he speeded around some of the curves, and undoubtedly there was considerable strain on the steaming qualities of the little engine. One day Galway failed to open the blow-off cock before starting out; this was needed to cleanse the boiler of residue from lime and other deposits in the water. The little engine foamed all the way up the hill to the extent that much of the water in the boiler went out the smokestack. Before the situation was brought under control, we had a terror-stricken engineer and fireman to deal with. Besides, I didn't feel secure next to Number 18 after walking back from the head-end of the cars where I set hand brakes to hold the train on the steep grade.

All we thought of was that the boiler might explode any minute. However, the fireman and I carefully shook the grates until all live coals in the firebox were dumped into the ashpan. After a check of the crown sheet was made showing it was not scorched, the injector was turned on to raise the water level in the boiler. Then the fireman shoveled some of the live coals from the ashpan back into the firebox to help build up the fire and steam pressure for continuing the climb up the hill, after I had released all of the hand brakes. This experience taught Galway a lesson that made him a more prudent engineer afterwards.

The track laborers living in boxcars at the supply yard were Croats, Macedonians, Serbians, Albians, Bulgarians, and Montenegrins. There were wild and bloody times when these feudal slavs obtained a large supply of moonshine likker. During the turbulence they would build a big fire and squat around it and then the "old world" ugliness would manifest itself. However, on the job they worked together as a team.

There were many steel trestles built. Instead of following the topographical contour of the hills the railroad was constructed to cut distance and curvature—a great feat of engineering. Track laying was a slow operation in those days. A locomotive with caboose behind and ties and rails on cars ahead would start out from the supply yard every other day. The next day

"The Coach of Fame," Pennsylvania car number 4418 at Travel Town, Griffith Park, Division of Parks and Recreation, City of Los Angeles. In the lower photo, left to right are William J. Woods, general sales manager, Pennsylvania Railroad; Charlie Atkins, travel town developer; and Jeff Keenan, who first conceived the idea of a memorial to railroad "greats." This one-time spacious dining car, which became "The Coach of Fame," was dedicated to those who made outstanding contributions to railroading in America.

The third person to become a member of the "Big Four of Railroad Romance" was Robert Taylor (Bob) McMillan. Here he receives the key to the Union Station at Portland from General Manager Jack Jones of the Portland Terminal Railroad on the arrival of Great Northern Train No. 407 at 1 p.m., August 13, 1955, Martha, his wife, at his side.

Author's wife, Helen, places a corsage on Martha's jacket while Bob and his brother, a rancher of Yakima, Washington, look on.

Oregon State Senator Rudie Wilhelm, Jr., takes the place of Governor Paul Patterson—who was out of the State at the time—greeting Bob at the train side.

dump cars containing crushed rock would be pushed ahead of the locomotive and the ballast dumped between the rails and ties that had been placed the previous day. This alternating operation, including the trip to and from Mullens every other day, continued for seven days each week. Ties had to be carried from cars for placement, followed by use of a hand-operated winch for handling rails, plus a lot of help from the laborers for placement on the ties. Another crew gauged the rails, spiked and fastened with fish plates—known as angle bars or rail joints today.

During 1907 I worked out of Bluefield, West Virginia, for the Norfolk & Western Railway, "braking coal drags" down the slopes of the Appalachians, which gave me a "veteran" status. Crawling over coal cars, setting up retainers, and tightening up hand brakes with a brake club was an experience I will always remember.

That fall I became restless and hired out to the Southern Railway as a locomotive fireman for service between Spencer, North Carolina, and Monroe, Virginia. My engineer signed me in as J. Keenan on the crew register at Monroe. The old engine crew dispatcher took it to mean Jefferson, a popular name in Virginia. In marking me on the engine crew board he cut it short to Jeff, a sobriquet that I am best known by.

While crossing Stillhouse trestle just north of Danville, Virginia, on my first trip I was reminded by my engineer that Joe Broady met his death there in "The Wreck of Old 97" just four years before. David Graves George, a hillbilly and former Southern Railway brakeman, who assisted in the rescue work at Stillhouse trestle, composed the ballad we know today as "The Wreck of Old 97."

Like most of the folk songs that have emanated from life, "The Wreck of Old 97" is based on a tragedy—the death of almost the entire crew. In this case the word "old" signifies endearment rather than age. The fast mail described as Old 97 had been operating about one year when she met the fate that the ballad writer used as his music score. The train started her meteoric rise in December, 1902, running between Washington, D.C. and Atlanta with expedited mail and express. Her discontinuance on January 6, 1907, had nothing to do with the wreck. Inasmuch as No. 97 carried no passengers, the run was discontinued when Congress failed to renew the appropriation for this special service.

LOCOMOTIVE FIREMAN AND ENGINEER

Being a fireman for the Southern Railway took me into the area where some of the Keenan family still resided in the eastern part of North Carolina. . .well remember crossing Stillhouse trestle, noted for "The Wreck of Old 97". . .arrived Columbus, Ohio, on Christmas Day of 1907. . .next day my name placed on firemen's roster of the Big 4, another adventure on the way. . .engineer for the Southern Indiana Railroad. . .firing "Mother Hubbards" for the Lehigh Valley.

I arrived in Columbus, Ohio, Christmas Day, 1907. The next day my name was placed on the firemen's roster of the Big 4 (now known as Penn Central). Within three months I was called occasionally to fire such trains as the Big 4 section of the 20th Century Limited and the Knickerbocker. Manually operated doors and a thirst for coal was the reputation of the Chautauqua-type locomotives which pulled those trains at that time. One was Number 373, built at the Brooks plant of the American Locomotive Works in 1904 and sent direct to the St. Louis World's Fair for display. With silver, gold and nickel trim, she was truly an eyecatcher, not only at the Fair but wherever she ran afterwards on the rails of the Big 4.

I will never forget the time I fired her for Bill Quinlan. It was Easter Sunday, March 27, 1908, and our train was the Cincinnati-New York section of the Century. In those days if the Century arrived late at Chicago, Cincinnati, or New York, the passengers were given a refund, but on that trip there was no need of a refund. I did not have to shovel down coal in the tender. We ran so fast that the swaying of the tender did it for me.

At MX Tower near Middletown, Ohio, a southbound freight delayed us for some reason I never did learn about. No lost time was made up until after leaving Dayton Union Station. Then Bill really took the bridle off. The train dispatcher, sensing what was about to happen, alerted all telegraph operators north of Fairborn to check our passing right to the second. The record shows we covered the three miles from Lilly Chapel to Georgesville at 101.3 miles per hour, the top speed ever made over 90-pound rails. Our locomotive on that memorable trip was Number 373, afterwards known as "The Speed Queen."

During 1908, a boiler explosion hospitalized my engineer, the head brakeman, and myself. I walked two miles to the next telegraph station to summon help which saved our lives, according to what the doctors said. The three of us were placed in a hospital ward next to each other. However, a few days passed before we discussed the accident. We learned later that thirty-six crown bolts were let loose because of the lack of water over that part of the crown sheet. Residue from lime and other deposits in the water had formed a crust that held back the water. Periodical cleansing of the boiler would have prevented the explosion.

Soon after my seventeenth birthday, after passing the required examination, I was employed by the Southern Indiana Railroad as a locomotive engineer and spent several months in the coal fields. When the miners left the pits I was furloughed. A few days later I hired out as a brakeman for service on the Little Miami division of the Pennsylvania Railroad. After making several trips between Columbus and Cincinnati, I was sent to Dayton to substitute for a switchman who had been injured. Although I did not apply for such service I was later informed that I was to be retained in Dayton. I resigned from the job after replacement.

Within a few days I visited an old friend, a station agent for the Lake Erie and Western (now part of the Norfolk & Western Railway) at Peru, Indiana. From the time that I first learned the Morse Code I never let the opportunity pass when I could let my fingers touch the keys of a telegraph instrument, and here was another opportunity. The yardmaster of the Chesapeake & Ohio of Indiana called on my friend while I was pounding away on the keys in the station and asked him if he knew of a person who could fill in as night yard clerk until the regular man returned from the hospital. After listening to their conversation that ended when my friend said he did not know of an available person, I offered my service until the regular man returned. My friend thought I was joking until I left with the yardmaster. He knew

I had run a locomotive and was in no dire need of money.

When I left Peru three months later, I must have wanted real action because on December 9, 1909, I was firing "Mother Hubbards" for the Lehigh Valley Railroad—the nickname for the camel-back type of locomotives with double cabs and the Wooten boiler. I was assigned to the extra board at Manchester, New York. Sometime later I was called to "deadhead" to Geneva to relieve a sick fireman. (It was on this local passenger train that I first met the girl whom I married years later. She was Helen White from a railroad family residing in Romulus, New York.)

The "Mother Hubbards" had two fire doors. A fireman had to learn to shovel coal into the firebox from the left side as well as the right side, and when the throttle was wide open, the fireman had to be fast with the scoop to keep up the steam pressure. Occasionally I heard it said that it took a strong back and a weak mind to fire a "Mother Hubbard." Perhaps my mind grew stronger and my back weaker at the time I resigned on April 12, 1910. However, there must have been something fascinating about firing a locomotive as I hired out again to the BIG 4 for service on the Ohio Division between Indianapolis, Cincinnati, Kankakee, and other terminals. Living conditions for a single man were inadequate so I resigned as of August 9, 1910.

BRAKEMAN—CONDUCTOR— MOTORMAN

Passenger brakeman on "The Abe Martin Line". . . crossing the International bridge. . .motorman for the Indiana Railroad. . .brakeman for the Chicago and Eastern Illinois Railroad. . .attempt made to rob C&EI train No. 18. . .visits with my father. . .disappointed in his efforts to have me enter University of Michigan to study journalism. . .marriage to Helen White, capstone of my life.

The next day, August 10, 1910, I was employed as a passenger brakeman in service between Indianapolis and Effingham, Illinois. The home terminal was Linton, Indiana. At that time the railroad was known as the Indianapolis Southern, which was about to be taken

The "Oregon Pony" provided a good setting for a picture of Bob, his brother, and his nephew, who was postmaster at Oswego, Oregon, at the time.

Monument created by the citizens of Centralia, Illinois, honoring Bob McMillan, dedicated on October 1, 1960. Grand Chief of the Brotherhood of Locomotive Engineers, Guy L. Brown, stands on one side with Bob on the opposite side.

The once-famous "Black Diamond Express." This picture was taken on the "Diamond's maiden run" between New York and Buffalo on May 18, 1895. (Photo courtesy of the Lehigh Valley Railroad)

Commemorative cover issued at Charleston, West Virginia, October 13, 1955, shows brakeman Keenan serving the old Coal & Coke Railway "50 years ago."

over by the Illinois Central System. However, the personality of the conductor and mine were in conflict so often that I resigned after two months.

The Indianapolis Southern was referred to as "The Abe Martin Line" because it passed through a corner of Brown County made famous by Frank McKinney "Kim" Hubbard, American caricaturist and humorist and creator of "Abe Martin" in the *Indianapolis News*.

As of October 29, 1910, I was employed by the Michigan Central Railroad (now part of Penn Central) to serve as a conductor-brakeman at Victoria Yard and to pilot whole trains across the International bridge as they arrived at Victoria Yard from St. Thomas, Ontario. Whole trains were generally for the Delaware, Lackawanna & Western (now Erie-Lackawanna Railway) interchange yard at Black Rock (now Buffalo). Some trains would be broken up at Victoria Yard and taken across the International Bridge without a caboose to ride in. Riding the rear freight car in below-zero weather to and from various railroad yards in Black Rock provided me with a preview of what I could expect during the coming winter.

Starting March 31, 1911, I gained a new experience serving the Indiana Union Traction Company as a motorman working out of Anderson and Tipton, Indiana, terminals. This electric railway operated luxurious trains such as the Muncie Meteor. It later became a component of the Indiana Railroad System, the largest of its kind in the country.

I never failed to visit Helen White during the interims of unemployment. If I had had an inkling of her plans to seek employment in Buffalo, I might have given a second thought about crossing the International Bridge in zero weather. After I terminated my service at Victoria Yard, I first learned of her plans. She was a beautiful and brilliant woman and a person of fairly even temperament. She and her sister Elizabeth were almost inseparable. Both were employed by Dr. George Gorrell, then superintendent of the Buffalo State Hospital. Although Elizabeth was older, Helen was placed in charge of the staff house. I learned later that she had the aptitude for taking over duties. In view of their togetherness, I almost always would invite Elizabeth to accompany us to dinners and to shows. She made good company for Helen and me.

I resigned my position as a motorman for the Indiana Union Traction Company on September 20, 1911, to spend some time with Helen before leaving for Danville, Illinois, where I was employed as a trainman on December 6, 1911, with prospects of promotion to conductor within the following year. Keeping up with the news relevant to railroads, I learned that the St. Louis-San Francisco Railway—better known as the Frisco—had openings for trainmen on the Chicago & Eastern Illinois Railroad, controlled by them.

In a circular dated August 7, 1902, the St. Louis-San Francisco Railway offered to purchase the C&EI preferred stock at $150 per share and common stock for $250 per share. This was accepted by the Porter interests, who sold their stock to the Frisco, which assumed control on October 1, 1902. Under date of May 1, 1903, control of the Frisco Lines passed to the Rock Island Lines, which thereby controlled the C&EI through Frisco.

In 1909, the Rock Island bowed out of the picture and the C&EI-Frisco reverted to its 1902 status. With both the C&EI-Frisco in financial trouble, the partnership broke up in 1913, each going its separate way. The opportunity for promotion to conductor, seniority rights respected, never took place during the rest of my employment with the C&EI. Under receivership, the C&EI restored the system that had been allowed to disintegrate. On January 1, 1918, the federal government took over the operation of the railroads and continued to manage them until March 1, 1920.

During the reign of Frisco, the syndicate operated fast mail trains between St. Louis and Chicago, Train Numbers 27 and 28 on the time tables. These trains carried large amounts of money on certain days. During March of 1913, four men left their horses tied to telegraph poles near the coal chute at Hillsboro, Illinois. When Number 28 stopped for coal four men approached the train. One covered the engineer and fireman, another started for the rear to cover the conductor and brakeman, while the other two bandits called to the mail clerks to open up or they would start shooting. I happened to be the brakeman that evening and upon dropping down from the rear car was greeted with what seemed to be a bullet that whistled past my ear. I lost no time in getting back into the car. Grabbing a rifle off the wall and gradually opening the side door gave me the advantage over the bandit making his way towards the rear car. A "lucky" shot disorganized the gang before an attempt was made to rifle the mail cars. Later we learned that three men on horseback crossed the Mississippi River below St. Louis on a ferry boat. The operator said he recognized Al Jennings as one of the three men.

While serving as a locomotive engineer for the Pacific Electric Railway, I had the opportunity of meeting Al in Hollywood during 1921. In discussing the Hillsboro affair, he neither confirmed nor denied being a member of the gang. However, he did state to other persons that he once failed in a train holdup that would have made him rich for the rest of his life. He also mentioned to them it was his last fling, and since he was not caught, he did not, until years later, let it become known because of the pardon granted to him by President Theodore Roosevelt in 1907. Al was living in Tarzana, California, in 1921.

As time passed, I thought of marriage to the one and only girl for me—and this moderated my yearning for further rambling about the country. Most of the tonnage hauled by the C&EI was coal, mined in many places along the line. From April to September of each year, most of the mines would close down, which greatly reduced the number of freight trains in operation. My summers were spent attending semesters at the University of Chicago and visiting Helen in Buffalo and my father in Michigan. He offered me the opportunity to study journalism at the University of Michigan and then enter the newspaper field. The lure of railroads took me back to the C&EI. Undoubtedly it wasn't the wisest decision, but who knows. . .

I took time off during October of 1915 to marry Helen White in Buffalo. We resided in Danville until December of 1917, and two of our daughters were born there.

While serving as a trainboy on trains of the Old Coal & Coke Railway, I learned that Uncle Joe Cannon served the Republican party for many years. From 1903 to 1911, he served as Speaker of the House of Representatives, ruling that body with an iron hand. I also learned that he was never seen without a stogie between his lips. The idea came to me then I could sell stogies to people who would prefer to buy three for a dime rather than pay five cents for one cigar. Naturally I called them "Uncle Joe's." The profit was about the same but it made for more sales. Years later I met Uncle Joe in Danville where he had resided for many years. I particularly observed that he still always had a stogie between his lips.

Other memories of those days include the need of funds before pay days; low wages would sometimes cause trainmen and enginemen to pawn their watches—that had passed the required inspection—to certain jewelers who would loan them up to ten dollars and charge a maximum of a dollar a month. If they did not have some kind of a replacement (generally an Ingersoll) they would buy one from me to use until they redeemed their good watch. Nevertheless, the Ingersoll generally kept good time, enabling them to get by. This meant frequently checking with standard time clocks in telegraph stations. While serving as a trainboy on different railroads I carried Ingersolls as part of my merchandise for sale, with one on each end of the watch chain across my vest. Most purchasers, however, preferred to buy Ingersolls carried in the pockets of my vest. The practice of pawning watches seemed to be prevalent among some trainmen and enginemen on all railroads, including the C&EI. For many years the Ingersoll sold for only one dollar.

The Elgin, Joliet & Eastern Railway, a subsidiary of the United States Steel Corporation that owned and/or worked several coal mines, operated their trains over the C&EI from points in Indiana and Illinois to Chicago Heights, where they connected with their own railroad. The EJ&E—also known as the Chicago Outer Belt—had physical connection with every railroad entering Chicago. In view of the prospects for slow promotion, and our nation becoming involved in World War I, I resigned my position with the C&EI. Although I was certified as exempt from the draft because of a wife and two daughters to support, I volunteered to serve in a semi-military capacity. During December of 1917, I arranged for them to go to New York State to reside with her sister Theresa at Kendaia.

RETURN TO CIVILIAN LIFE

Dispatching trains. . .train service as conductor, trainmaster and assistant superintendent. . .during interim handling control levers of "juice jacks". . . family and I moved to Portland, Oregon, May 26,

Top: Jeff at the throttle in the cab of C. K. Holliday. shaking hands with E. R. Lemmon, Area Manager, Main Street, Disneyland, on October 28, 1955.

Left: Pass No. 5 certifying C. J. Keenan as an honorary vice president of the Santa Fe & Disneyland Railroad—signed by Walt Disney.

SANTA FE & DISNEYLAND R. R.

1955
VOID AFTER DATE

This is to certify that

C. J. KEENAN

IS AN HONORARY VICE PRESIDENT OF
THE SANTA FE & DISNEYLAND RAILROAD

No. 005

Walt Disney

35

1899610

My wife, Helen, and I left Portland for the East during August of 1957, stopping over enroute at various places of interest, especially at Lockport, New York, our old home city from 1919 to 1926, to visit relatives and friends. Then we went on to New York City, where Andrew Fleischman, retired customs agent for the New York Central, took us through Wall Street and all over lower Manhattan, including the Chase National Bank Museum and the Cunard Building where Andy had his office for many years. From New York City we headed for Roanoke, Virginia, to attend the National convention of the National Railway Historical Society. We stayed at the Roanoke Hotel, owned and operated by the Norfolk and Western Railway. The service there was peerless and the convention was a success from start to finish. The train trips were enjoyed, especially from Roanoke to Matoaka via the Norfolk and Western and return to Roanoke via The Virginian Railway.

1926. . .serving in various capacities for the Southern Pacific Lines. . .rate expert and later revenue auditor on the staff of Public Utilities Commissioner of Oregon. . .retired June 1, 1957. . .during the Casey Jones ceremonies at Jackson, Tennessee, April 29, 1950, the foundation was established for the Casey Jones Fellowship, better known as the Big 4 of Railroad Romance.

Returning to civilian employment the latter part of 1918, I was rejoined by my family. My first employment was as train dispatcher for the Elmira, Corning & Waverly Railway, a component of the Erie Railroad serving at Big Flats, New York. My next role was dispatching trains for the Rochester, Lockport & Buffalo Railway during 1919. Then, 1920-21 brought a new experience for me in California handling the control levers of Pacific Electric Railway "juice jacks," switching Hollywood and other points on the Western Division. My home terminal was Sherman, now West Hollywood.

Later, in 1921, I returned East to serve the International Railway as a conductor, trainmaster, and assistant superintendent, respectively, with headquarters in Lockport, New York. The freight movement of this line was later returned to the operation of the Erie Railroad which owned the trackage between North Tonawanda and Lockport. This abolished some of the official duties of International Railway personnel.

In May of 1926, my family and I moved to Portland, Oregon. There were four daughters then, two having been born in Lockport. Thirteen years of serving in various capacities with the Southern Pacific Lines, coupled with knowledge gained by attending semesters at the University of Chicago at Chicago, prepared me as a rate expert and later as a revenue auditor on the staff of the Public Utilities Commissioner of Oregon, where I served from 1941 until retirement as of June 1, 1957. This allowed me full time for the development of the National Railroad Hall of Fame and Museum, Inc., to which I have been dedicated for many years.

It was a real pleasure to serve the P.U.C. of Oregon. An employe showing the proper initiative and application was given a wide latitude for performance; on the other hand, if he elected not to pursue the duties he was employed to perform, it soon showed up in his compendium. I always found the officers and other employes dedicated and fair to work with. Actually, I did not retire, other than to have my name removed from the payroll, leaving me free to establish a national railroad hall of fame and museum.

NARHFAM
THE NATIONAL RAILROAD HALL OF FAME AND MUSEUM

Dedicated most of my life to that part of our American heritage. . .during the past, majority of railroad officials approved of such a project as Narhfam, but never got around to appropriating funds for same. . . twenty-two persons are enshrined in the Hall of Fame, starting with Abraham Lincoln. . .nine persons are enshrined in the Hall of Romance, starting with Casey Jones.

NARHFAM stands for the National Railroad Hall of Fame and Museum, Inc., founded on July 4, 1950. It is America's historical shrine dedicated to persons who have made significant contributions to American railroads of the past and the future; and it is a foundation maintained for the education and pleasure of all people.

The building of the American railroad system was one of the greatest dramas of modern times. Unlike the Republic itself, whose founding can be dated well enough for all practical and symbolic purposes as of July 4, 1776, the American railroad system cannot be said to have a birthday. For many years it existed only in the minds of a few visionaries who, try as they might, could make little impression on the great mass of Americans, then charmed by the wonders of canals.

It was during the summer of 1925 that I discussed the founding of a national railroad hall of fame and museum with R. H. Aishton, who was then president of the old American Railroad association with headquarters at Chicago. A few months later he informed me there was not enough sentiment for promotion at that time. At the Chicago Railroad Fair in 1948, I discussed the same subject with Carlton Corliss, then manager of Public Relations, Association of American Railroads, Washington, D.C. He said he had talked to several railroad executive about building a railroad hall of fame and museum in the District of Columbia. The majority approved such a project, but never got around to appropriating funds for it.

A year later, Mr. Corliss urged me to give it another try. Thanks to James Symes, then president of the Pennsylvania Railroad, a refurbished dining car was donated and designated "The Coach of Fame." When the "coach" was found to be inadequate, it was donated to Travel Town, a division of the Department of Recreation and Parks, City of Los Angeles.

As of June 1, 1958, NARHFAM became a non-profit, tax-exempt and educational corporation for the procurement and maintenance of buildings and railway coaches as a museum and historical shrine relating to persons recognized for their achievements in railroad development —and for the selection and enshrinement of such persons themselves. It is further dedicated to the collection, display, and maintenance of pictures, plaques, monuments, biographical sketches and other items concerning such persons, and exhibiting the same to the public. None of the income or assets acquired inure to any private individual or group. The corporation is only an instrument for directing the advancement of NARHFAM.

NATIONAL RAILWAY HISTORICAL SOCIETY

Organized Pacific Northwest Chapter. . .First issue of The Trainmaster. . .track laid at Oaks Park for locomotives. . ."golden spike" driven to mark opening of "short line" for locomotives donated to the City of Portland. . .Mark (Buck) Grayson, master of ceremonies.

As of March 16, 1955, I organized the first chapter of the National Railway Historical Society west of Topeka, Kansas, and named it the Pacific Northwest. The first meeting was held in the Union Station at Portland. Two of our charter members were Stewart Hall Holbrook and Harry Bedwell. Mr. Holbrook, informal historian and writer, was the author of *The Story of American Railroads* and *The Life of Jim Hill* and many other books. Mr. Bedwell wrote many stories for *Railroad Magazine*, *Saturday Evening Post* and other periodicals.

The first issue of *The Trainmaster*—newsletter of the Pacific Northwest Chapter—was issued as of March 31, 1956. Until a more capable editor came forward to take over the job, I continued as the editor.

The late Dick Fagan, who was Mill Ends editor of the *Oregon Journal*, Portland, published in his column of October 17, 1956, the following: "Some of most nostalgic people in the world are those who loved the old steam locomotives, the interurbans and cable cars. And no one keeps better track of the passing of these things than C.J. (Jeff) Keenan, editor of *The Trainmaster* of the Pacific Northwest Chapter of the National Railway Historical Society. Here are some excerpts from the last issue:

"Oldest interurban electrical railway in the United States discontinued operations into downtown Portland the morning of September 17, 1956. Car No. 4018 of the Portland Traction made the last run over the downtown loop at 1:20 a.m. Sixty-three years ago on February 16, 1893, the first interurban left Portland's west side for Oregon City, 14 miles away. And your editor has not yet become addicted to the yowl of the diesel horn. It is a far cry from the 'whippoorwill' of Casey Jones' whistle and the captivating chimes of Uncle Billy Richardson's whistle which stopped the mountaineers in their tracks to catch the last echo."

Sixty railroad section hands cheerfully swung 10-pound mauls and wrestled railroad ties on Saturday, December 7, 1957, to lay 330 feet of track for free on their day off. Although only forty were expected, 60 members of the Brotherhood of Maintenance of Way employes turned out to build the rail line at Oaks Amusement Park. The spur track will be the temporary location of Union Pacific No. 3203, Spokane, Portland & Seattle No. 700, and locomotives of other carriers, serving Portland and Oregon.

The morning air rang with the sharp clang of sledge hammers on spikes as the track layers accomplished the job in 90 minutes amid a holiday atmosphere of civic good will. Rails and ties were donated by the Union Pacific and Southern Pacific railroads. The spur was connected to the nearby Portland Traction Company tracks. Two weeks later the locomotives were moved in. (In railroad tradition a "golden spike" was driven to mark the opening of the "short line.")

HAROLD S. LUDLOW was born, April 22, 1886, in Cleveland, Ohio, and died, September 22, 1959, in Vermilion, Ohio. The Vermilion village flag flew at half mast until the funeral services were completed. Harold Ludlow attained widespread fame for his hobby of collecting photographs and sounds of trains, particularly of the almost obsolete "iron horse"—steam locomotives. His collection of photographs and little-known facts was one of the finest in Ohio, and his motion pictures and sound recordings were almost unparalleled. He acted as narrator for an album of tape-recorded sounds he collected from thirty New York Central trains—which was issued by Folkway Records. The wheels of Mr. Ludlow's recorder turned in tempo with the trains he loved. He sometimes said, "when the steam locomotive is finally gone, I will lay down my camera." Mr. Ludlow retired in 1951 after forty years with the Ohio Bell Telephone Company. He was general plant supervisor of the Cleveland main office. Top (left) picture shows him with a Graflex camera in the cab of Nickle Plate—New York, Chicago & St. Louis, No. 709, on October 8, 1957.

Top right shows him with wire recorders in May of 1958. Wire recorders predate the tape recorders. (All the pictures in this book taken at Huron and Vermilion by Harold Ludlow. He donated them to the National Railroad Hall of Fame and Museum, for which we shall always be grateful to his memory.)

June of 1963 was an enterprising month for me. I left Portland soon after the first of the month for Buffalo, New York, having been appointed by the directors of NARHFAM as ambassador for presenting the Certificate of Award—enshrining Sir Casimir Stanislaus Gzowski—to W. C. Bowra, General Manager, Great Lakes Region, Canadian National Railways, on the International Bridge over the Niagara River, connecting Fort Erie, Ontario, with Buffalo, New York. The Ceremony took place on June 8, 1963. I next went to Columbus, Ohio, to present the Certificate of Award—enshrining James J. Andrews—to Governor Rhodes, as was planned by the Ohio State Historical Society.

That evening I left for Phoenix, Arizona, where I was to attend the national convention of the American Topical Association. My roomette on the Imperial from Kansas City to Phoenix—over the Rock-Island-Southern Pacific route—was comfortable. The food served in the diner was delectable. The trip was enjoyable and the stopover at El Paso was appreciated for exercise, as you might suspect. Here I am standing alongside the "Golden West," one of the Pullman cars of the Imperial consist. Lower right picture was taken by August H. Pritzlaff, Jr., railroad enthusiast, also interested in railway philately.

PACIFIC NORTHWEST CHAPTER

NATIONAL RAILWAY HISTORICAL SOCIETY

THE TRAINMASTER

| Volume 1 - Number 1 | Portland, Oregon | March 31, 1956 |

CHAPTER NOTES

Harry Bedwell, one of our charter members, passed away on October 4, 1955. Mourned by his widow Lorraine and members of this chapter, he will be missed by millions of readers. Harry Bedwell ranked second to none as a railroad fictioneer. Railroad Magazine, Saturday Evening Post, and other periodicals published his many stories, most of which have become classics. As a small tribute to a great author Railroad Magazine reprinted one of them, "Sun and Silence" in the April issue. His close friend, Bill Knapke, found in his desk an unpublished manuscript, "The Sound of an Avalanche", and sold it to The Saturday Evening Post for a price that ran well into four figures. The next issue of Railroad Magazine will carry another famous Bedwell yarn from long ago, "On the Night Wire".

Honorable Richard L. Neuberger, United States Senator from Oregon, whose by-line is railroads, is a charter member.

Damon Trout, widely known for his interest in railroadiana, has applied for membership. Damon has his own transportation museum at Cedar Mill, which includes a cable car formerly operated in San Francisco.

PASSING PARADE

March was quite a month for Portland. First was the arrival of Lucius Beebe and Charles Clegg in their ornate private railroad car. Finishing a tour of the United States, they're on the way back to home in Virginia City, Nevada. Author Stewart Holbrook, their host here, is a charter member of this chapter. Messrs. Beebe and Clegg say that the private car is the only one in the country owned by those who ride in it.

Next the futuristic aerotrain rolled into Portland over the Union Pacific. The present locomotive, designed for flat country, needed a helper over the Blue Mountains of eastern Oregon.

A few days later part of San Francisco's local color - a cable car passed through Portland to be transplanted in Forest Grove. It will be added to W. W. McCredy's "car barn".

AMERICAN RAILROAD SHRINE

One of the most stirring events in the romance of railroads will take place within a few days when the most celebrated of all 10-wheelers, "Old 382", will come down from the Cumberland mountains over the "Dixie Route" to its lasting resting place at the American Railroad Shrine in Jackson, Tennessee. "Old 382" carried Casey Jones to his death the morning of April 30, 1900, at Vaughan, Mississippi. The shrine, to be dedicated on April 30, will enthrone "Old 382" and also Casey's old home.

First issue of *The Trainmaster*.

Delivery of UP 3203 and SP&S 700 to the City of Portland, Bureau of Parks, at Oaks Park was made on January 14, 1958. Master of ceremonies was Mark (Buck) Grayson, Administrative Assistant to Commissioner Ormond Bean, who gave a brief talk about the nature of the ceremony. Introduction and remarks were made by George H. Baker, Division Superintendent, now General Manager, Union Pacific, and L.W. Albertson, Vice President, Spokane, Portland & Seattle, who presented to Commissioner Bean documents giving the city title to the locomotives. Introduction and remarks were also made by Harry Buckley, Superintendent of Parks; Ormond Bean, City Commissioner; Bob Hocks, Oaks Park Area Advisory Committee.

As President of Pacific Northwest Chapter, National Railway Historical Society, I also made introductory remarks as follows: "Thank you, Mr. Grayson, and other distinguished gentlemen. It is with deep gratification in behalf of the members of NRHS that I address you today on this auspicious occasion. In these days of fantasy that seems to have overcome many adults as well as the young, it is refreshing to be present at an event that will benefit our people and enhance railroad history. This is another real start to preserve the 'Iron Horse' for generations to come.

"Railroads serving Portland and not eventually represented by exhibiting a steam or electric locomotive will have waived acclamation, because this is an exhibition that people of the nation will tour—not detour.

"I deeply appreciate the honor of having been chosen to participate with City Commissioner Ormond Bean in driving the 'golden spike' to connect the rails to hold the first locomotives of the exhibit. May its success be constant.

"If railroads created a dreamworld for boys of my generation, and they most certainly did, it was merely incidental. Of all industries, the railroads have made the greatest contribution to the unparalleled development of this country, and to its defense, and in the constant elevation of its standard of living."

Excerpts from the *Oregon Journal* of January 12, 1958, follow: "Two railroad steam locomotives will make their last trip Tuesday to a new home at Oaks Park where the city will display them as transportation relics. The Park Bureau eventually hopes to develop property next to Oaks Park into a transportation museum which would include these old engines. On hand, too,

will be members of railroad historical clubs and retired railroaders who have pulled the throttle of these two locomotives. The public is invited. Before the engines are pushed onto their storage track, Jeff Keenan, president of the Pacific Northwest Chapter, National Railway Historical Society, will drive a gilded spike at the head end of the track."

Excerpts from the *Locomotive Engineer*, published by the Brotherhood of Locomotive Engineers in the March 14, 1958, issue follow: "When two veteran steam locomotives were pushed onto a siding at Oaks Park early this year, Portland, Oregon, was moving towards the transportation it wants and some Brotherhood members were having their memories jogged. The UP engine was built by Baldwin at Philadelphia in 1905. She made her debut at La Grande, Oregon, and later was assigned to passenger service between Portland and Pendleton, Spokane and Seattle. She was used to pull branch line trains before her retirement in 1953. The SP&S No. 700 was built by Baldwin in 1938. She was used in passenger service between Portland and Spokane until 1956, when she became the last of the company's steam locomotives to be retired.

"I operated SP&S No. 700 thousands of miles through daylight and darkness with her gleaming bright headlight buffeting the night to show a clear track ahead," said Neil C. Ryan, Division 758. Ryan, now eighty-six, retired in 1944. He was present at the dedication ceremony at Oaks Park along with other railroaders, civic officials, and railfans.

"Prime mover in Portland efforts to establish a transportation museum is Jeff Keenan, president of the Pacific Northwest Chapter of the National Railway Historical Society. The city agreed to develop the museum on a site adjacent to the present location of the locomotives . . .A.F. (Al) Zimmerman, General Chairman, Brotherhood of Locomotive Engineers, Northwestern District, Union Pacific, has also been active in the program, even helping lay track on which the venerable locomotives now rest."

HONORS

Enshrinement of Sir Casimir Stanislaus Gzowski in the Railroad Hall of Fame. . .Jesus Garcia, locomotive engineer who saved the city of Narcozari from destruction.

The *Buffalo Courier-Express* carried the following article in the June 5, 1963, issue: "An event of railroad interest will take place high over the Niagara River Saturday afternoon. A special Canadian National Railways train will halt midway across the International Bridge between Fort Erie and Black Rock for ceremonies enshrining the span's engineer in the National Railroad Hall of Fame.

"Sir Casimir Stanislaus Gzowski, a Polish nobleman who emigrated to the U.S. in 1833 and later to Canada where he died in 1898, was a civil engineer whose several railroad jobs included construction of the International Bridge in 1870-1873.

"C.J. Jeff Keenan, a former Buffalonian and retired railroader who founded the Hall of Fame in 1950, and Chairman of the Board will present the Certificate of Award to W.C. Bowra, General Manager of the Great Lakes Region of the Canadian National Railways. The ceremony will take place approximately over the international boundary in the Niagara River when the special train reaches that spot after departing from the Fort Erie depot at 2: P.M.

"The train will include a specially constructed open gondola car equipped with seats for participants. Among them will be Mayor John M. Teal of Fort Erie who has invited Mayor Chester Kowal of Buffalo to participate. Also invited are a grandson, great granddaughter and great-grandson of Sir Casimir, all residents of Canada.

"The consist of the special three car train will also include two cars sent from Montreal by President Gordon of the Canadian National Railways. One is the Caribou, a parlor car ordinarily operated in the International Limited between Montreal and Toronto. The other is the Atlantic, a compartment car of the regular consist for carriage of Queen Elizabeth and the Duke of Edinburgh while traveling throughout Canada, also for carriage of Winston Churchill and other notables. The Atlantic was in the Royal Train consist which operated throughout the United States a few years ago."

As of June 1, 1957, directors of NARHFAM voted to include the great railroad builders and persons memorable in railroad history of Canada and Mexico. We have our Casey Jones who gave his life in the line of duty to save others. To live in the way of men, to spend one's time watching selfish interests, to think of personal safety when many others may die be-cause of this attitude—the average man may thus be swayed to his own interests. But November 7th is the anniversary date of the death of a truly different man, one for whom "nature might stand up and say to all the World"—this was a man—Jesus Garcia who served the Nacozari Railroad of Mexico as a locomotive engineer. This railroad for many years was a component of the Southern Pacific Lines.

MEETING OTHER EMINENT PERSONS

John J. Barriger, "Traveling Freight Agent and President". . .Colonel Elliott White Springs, head of the Springs organization. . .H.W. Close, head of the Springs textile creation. . .Walt Disney, trainboy to fabulous career of showmanship.

I have had the pleasure of meeting and associating with many people in the past, people eminent in their professional or special fields of endeavor. Among them is John W. Barriger. After retirement as director of the Pittsburgh & Lake Erie Railroad he was drafted as president of the St. Louis-San Francisco Railway and a short time later as president of the Missouri-Kansas-Texas (Katy Railroad). He preferred to be known as "Traveling Freight Agent and President," for his travels throughout the territory.

We were students of railroad consolidations. Some of his addresses related to "Aggiornomen-to," especially at the meeting of the Trans Missouri-Kansas Shippers Board at the Hotel President, Kansas City, Missouri, January 19, 1966. My concept was for the formation of six transcontinental systems, they to equally own as stockholders only, the railroads operating in the New England states. I believe the present predicament of many U.S. railroads now proves that my theory was sound.

Col. Elliott White Springs became head of the Springs organization upon the death of his father, Leroy, in 1931. Owning a small railroad amused the Colonel and he had a lot of fun with the short line as it (Lancaster & Chester) passed through its most colorful period. Colonel Springs named twenty-nine vice presidents to the line's board of directors, one for each mile of track. Gypsy Rose Lee was named for un-

The occasion here celebrated was the donation of two locomotives to the City of Portland by the U.P. and S.P.&S. railroads, Jan. 14, 1958. There was no hole drilled for the spike to fall in—Jeff had to go about it like a gandy dancer and aim at the head of the spike with force enough to keep driving it into the crosstie. There were a lot of old-time railroaders around to see how he performed. Their count was seven strikes. Union Pacific No. 3203 was there waiting for the "yard goat"—switcher to shove her to her berth.

Spokane, Portland & Seattle No. 700 was not far behind, ready to proudly display her beautiful form. (Picture of No. 700 unavailable so a picture of a sister locomotive No. 702 is used.)

Southern Pacific Lines locomotive No. 4449 kept company with locomotives, Union Pacific No. 3203, and Spokane, Portland and Seattle No. 700 from 1958 to November 14, 1974, when it was moved out of Oaks Park, for equipment overhaul at the Burlington Northern Roundhouse, Portland. It was loaned to the American Bicentennial Commission to pull a 24-car "Freedom Train" through various states as part of the U.S. Bicentennial activities, in 1975-76. The train will carry national documents and artifacts as a mobile museum. It is interesting to note that Ormond Bean, then City Commissioner of Portland, and Jeff Keenan, then President of the Pacific Northwest Chapter, National Railway Historical Society, were the prime movers in securing the locomotives from the S. P., S. P. & S., and U. P., for the City of Portland.

veiling and came to Lancaster in the mid-1950's when the new L. & C. depot was dedicated.

Chartered in 1873 as the Cheraw & Chester Railway, the new line was part of the early development of a rail link between coastal cities of the East and the produce markets of the middle West—an effort to channel to Eastern ports the goods being floated down the Mississippi River to New Orleans.

In 1896, Colonel Leroy Springs bought the line at public auction for $25,000. He secured a new charter, renamed the line the Lancaster & Chester Railroad, and set about ways to increase traffic over the 29-mile route. One of his first acts was to name as the railroad's directors the merchants who supplied traffic to the new line. Colonel Leroy found that his newly acquired railroad had some disadvantages. Because the tracks were narrow gauge, it couldn't interchange carloads with the main lines serving the nation. His railroad locomotives burned wood and all the coal mines were on broad gauge lines. It was not economical to reload the coal cars. To solve his problem, Colonel Leroy knew that he had to go to broad-gauge tracks. He bonded the Lancaster & Chester Railroad to the Southern Railway, borrowed $125,000 and made the switch to broad gauge.

Colonel Elliott White Springs died in 1959 and was succeeded by his son-in-law, H.W. Close, who now heads the Springs textile organization. Like the colonel, Bill Close has a special fondness for the L. & C. and its long and colorful history. A recent letter from Close to members of the L. & C.'s directors bears this out:

"For a time last August the L. & C. was a washout. The problem was rain. The heaviest rains in 60 years washed away six miles of ballast. Service to Orr's siding, Knox's Station and Chester was suspended for three weeks. But you can't keep a good road down. L. & C. crews hauled in 100 cars of ballast, drove piling, installed corrugated steel, tamped, resealed—and The Springmaid Line was back in business.

"Indeed, the L. & C. progressed. We added 6,100 feet of side track, relaid six miles of main line with 112-pound rail, and reprinted the dining car menu. We also added a pickup that runs on highway or rail and has compressed air attachments for driving spikes, tightening bolts and shooing cows, politicians and foreign imports off the right-of-way.

"Your L. & C. pass for 1934 is attached. Our box lunches and ballast are packed. We await your inspection."

Walt Disney and I were trainboys working out of Chicago—he on a Santa Fe run to Kansas City. My run was on the Baltimore and Ohio to Zanesville, Ohio. His earnings helped to pay his tuition in art school at Chicago. The life and works of Walt Disney, his eminence, and the impacts of his artistry and showmanship on his times, are not readily encompassed in dates and data. His fabulous career bursts out of conventional bounds with events of historic consequence in motion pictures and television, as well as those of personal nature.

In 1923, a tall, lean son of the Midwest came unheralded to Hollywood, mecca of the movies. His equipment for his chosen profession consisted largely of $40 in a well-worn suit and a boundless ambition hitched to a fantastic imagination. Pooling funds with brother Roy, and with an additional $500 borrowed from an uncle, Walt was in business. With the opening of the beautiful Burbank Studio in 1940, the Disney production personnel soared to over 1,000 artists, animators, story men and technicians. They were literally guided at every turn by the indefatigable man of ideas and fantastic works. Creations of his own and brilliant adaptations of the great classic fables and fairy tales were produced with incredible industry and creative energy. They took the entertainment world by storm; made the Disney name more illustrious. It became a synonym for what was unique and best in bringing laughter and buoyancy to people of all nations.

Walt's Cinema-scope-technicolor, "The Great Locomotive Chase," is steeped in the Disney brand of authenticity that holds motion picture audiences so successfully. He left nothing undone to achieve the ultimate in believability so that this magnificent story, vibrant with action and suspense, could be relived on the screen in every fascinating detail. The picture is based on an incredible historic incident. James J. Andrews, a Union spy, drove deep into the heart of the Confederacy, stole two freight cars of a passenger and freight train standing at Big Shanty and raced back through Georgia toward his own lines in a well-calculated attempt to ruin the South's strategically vital transport system and end the war far ahead of time. He failed because William A. Fuller, an indomitable Confederate train conductor who didn't hesitate to begin the chase on foot, caught and stopped the Andrews Raiders in their tracks. The Andrews raid shook the nation when it became public knowledge that for a period of eight hours the outcome of the Civil War may have hung on the spinning drive wheels of two fast locomotives, the "General" and the "Texas."

Military experts later agreed that the "war between the states" would have ended one to two years sooner if Andrews had not made two blunders. He failed to burn the Etowah River bridge and rejected the advice of Engineer Knight that they stop and disable the Yonah to prevent further pursuit.

There is a sequel to "The Great Locomotive Chase" relating to "The Ghost of Allatoona Gap." Here on October 5, 1864, less than a month after the fall of Atlanta, some of the most desperate fighting of the war took place. Union forces had captured the Western & Atlantic Railroad at this point and General Sherman had left a large army on the heights above the tracks. Confederate General Hood attacked fiercely. The gap, a few miles north of Big Shanty, where "The Great Locomotive Chase" started, on a wild and God-forsaken mountain top, is said to be haunted by the wraith of a Western & Atlantic brakeman whose body lies where he fell as a Confederate soldier, near the rails. It is said the brakeman was the first to fall during the battle. Only a few hours before, he had left his train—which was bottled up beyond the gap—obtained a rifle, and joined General Hood's army. Trainmen declare the "ghost" of the fallen brakeman jumps from the cut onto their trains or engines and then fades away. His grave is enclosed with an iron fence, a small tombstone rising above the crushed rock mound.

Serving the Southern Railway as a locomotive fireman at the age of fifteen between Spencer, North Carolina, and Monroe, Virginia, during 1907, there were days I was free to travel south on the Southern to see what the country looked like. On one of those trips I got off the train at Cornelia, Georgia, and rode a passenger train of the Tallulah Falls Railway between that town and Franklin, North Carolina, a six-hour trip, returning to board a Southern train back to Spencer. I kind of took a liking to the little railroad and as a boy dreamed of owning such a

railroad. This small line continued to be a favorite. That could have had something to do with Walt Disney scouting the line for production of his Cinema-scope-technicolor, "The Great Locomotive Chase." I made sure that the Tallulah Falls Railway was saluted by the National Railroad Hall of Fame and Museum on its day, September 4, 1959, at the Oregon Centennial Exposition. Freight traffic moving by trucks over improved highways forced the abandonment of the carrier as of June 14, 1961.

ENSHRINEMENTS—HALL OF FAME

Twenty-two persons honored starting with Abraham Lincoln and continuing on to Sir Donald Alexander Smith.

Since retiring from the payroll of the Public Utilities Commission of Oregon, June 1, 1957, I have given full time to the advancement of NARHFAM. There are two classifications, one for the great locomotive and railroad builders who are elected and enshrined in the Hall of Fame, the other for persons memorable in railroad history, who are enshrined in the Hall of Romance. Persons enshrined in the Hall of Fame are as follows:

ABRAHAM LINCOLN as of July 4, 1958. Certificate of Award reposes in the Lincoln National Life Foundation at Fort Wayne, Indiana. Nine months before he was nominated for the Presidency of the United States, he climbed to the top of a high cliff at Council Bluffs, Iowa, and looked westward. As he looked over those wide-spreading plains, he symbolized America. For America, too, was looking to the West and dreaming of its future. On July 1, 1862, he signed the enabling Act that created the Central Pacific and Union Pacific railroads.

COLONEL JOHN STEVENS as of July 4, 1958. Certificate of Award reposes in the Official Library of the Penn Central Transportation Company. His true interest lay in applying steam to land transportation. Pursuing that goal he won greater distinction as the "Father of American Railroads."

Within the photograph, on the clearance form:

CN   CANADIAN NATIONAL RAILWAYS   CN-710
      CLEARANCE   8-61

STATION Fort Erie B1   June 8   19 63

TRAIN   Extra 8113 East

ORDERS FOR
YOUR TRAIN {   NIL
ARE

THE NEXT TRAIN AHEAD FROM THIS STATION LEFT AT _____

OK AT ____ 200 pm.   A Fleater

        DISPATCHER   OPERATOR

Top: Compartment car, Atlantic, Right: Clearance issued
by Canadian National Railways to Extra 8113 East for trip
over the bridge.

Left: John W. Barriger. Below: Personal letter received from Mr. Barriger when he was president of the Pittsburgh & Lake Erie Railroad Company. On his annual trips across the country, Mr. Barriger always invited people, especially shippers and their traffic personnel, to a "Katy" dinner at which time he was able to discuss at first hand ways and means to provide better service.

THE PITTSBURGH & LAKE ERIE RAILROAD COMPANY

THE LAKE ERIE & EASTERN RAILROAD COMPANY

JOHN W. BARRIGER
PRESIDENT

PITTSBURGH 19, PA.

November 17, 1964

Mr. C. J. Keenan
5114 S. W. Scholls Ferry Road
Portland, Oregon - 97225

Dear Mr. Keenan:

Your good company added greatly to the pleasure of the P&LE luncheon in Portland on Thursday, October 22, and I appreicated your note of good wishes upon my prospective retirement on December 31 that was awaiting my return here.

Your fine work for the railroad industry, through your National Railroad Hall of Fame and Museum, is recognized and appreciated by your friends throughout the country.

It will always be a pleasure to see you whenever my future travels may take my to Portland, as I hope they will continue to do in each successive year.

Very sincerely yours,

LANCASTER AND CHESTER RAILWAY COMPANY

EDITORIAL
Oregon Journal, February 5, 1957

RAILROAD WITH a SENSE of HUMOR

One usually doesn't think of a railroad having a sense of humor, competition being what it is in these days
of fast planes, wide highways and open
rivers, but down in South Carolina there
is a short line that finds time to laugh
a bit while counting its profits.
It claims to be the first railroad in
South Carolina to be 100 per cent dieselized,
but its fame doesn't rest on that accomplish-
ment. Rather, a glance at the roster of its
officersconvinces the reader that life is
something less than serious at all times to
the management. Like other railroads, the
Lancaster & Chester Railway company has a
president, a whole flock of vice presidents,
a general manager and other officials, including a news butcher.
Unlike other railroads, however, the L&C
assigns some of its vice presidents to
specific duties. For instance, one VP of
prominence is James Mongomery Flagg, whose
reputation as an artist surely overshad-
ows his accomplishments as a railroader. But
next on the list is Adm. "Bull"Halsey of
World War II naval fame. And then the clin-
cher; Gypsy Rose Lee is vice president in
charge of unveiling, surely a natural for
the queen of burlesque. One more name deserves mention; Lucius Beebe, gourmet and
Virginia City, Nev., editor, is vice president in charge of the internal audit.
In addition to being proud of having the
first fully dieselized road in the state,
should lay claim to being a railroad with
a sense of humor and a talent for selecting
the right persons for unusual duties.

Top: Editorial, *Oregon Journal*, Portland, February 5, 1957.

Left: Colonel Springs and his family at the rear of their private car, "Caboose." The "caboose" was equipped for fast
passenger service.

49

Grenville M. Dodge was chief engineer of the Union Pacific during most of the construction. From 1870 to 1897 he was a director.

The Central Oregon Railroad War

Into the Central Oregon country, one day, went a genial sportsman, one John F. Sampson, who carried more poles and reels and trout flies than had ever before been seen on the Deschutes, a notable trout stream. Sampson appeared to be carrying a lot of cash, too, and so taken was he with this sportsman's paradise that he bought options on wild lands and ranches all over the place. Then he suddenly disappeared.

In Portland at this time lived William Nelson, who owned controlling interest in a non-existent railroad called the Oregon Trunk. A little surveying had been done for this road, long before, up the east bank of the Deschutes River. Otherwise it existed wholly on paper when Nelson was surprised to be approached by the mysterious sportsman, Mr. Sampson, and all but stunned a few days later when Mr. Sampson and he met in a city park and Sampson paid him $150,000 in good legal tender for his stock in the Oregon Trunk.

Right on the heels of this astounding transaction, the stranger appeared again, this time under his right name, which was John F. Stevens. He was none other than the former chief engineer of the Panama Canal, the same engineer who had discovered a fine lost pass through the Rockies, as the result of Blackfoot Indians telling him to watch for the trail that herds of bison took through the Rockies. His employer was Jim Hill, for whom he acted as agent and chief engineer. Stevens announced that Mr. Hill was about to construct a railroad from the Columbia River up the Deschutes River and to an unknown town of Central Oregon called Bend.

But Mr. Harriman knew very well that Bend was more the terminus Mr. Hill had in mind for his seemingly Oregon railroad. Hill, he was certain, meant to build to Bend, right enough, and so on in a direct line to San Francisco. It would not do to leave Central Oregon alone with Mr. Hill for a moment. To parallel Hill's Oregon Trunk, Harriman moved a gigantic crew into the area and they proceeded to make grade and lay track up the west bank of the Deschutes, calling their line the Deschutes Railroad.

George W. Boschke, who had built the famous sea wall at Galveston, Texas, was in charge of the Harriman forces. And now while much of the West watched with increasing excitement, the two great men on Western railroading engaged in what proved to be the last of the formidable railroad-construction wars. All supplies, even hay, had to be packed in for the huge crews working for each company. In the narrow Deschutes Canyon, in a cleft in high hills of rock, the gangs carried on a war by exploding dynamite charges to interfere with the opposing faction. Men were killed, some by boulders that mysteriously started rolling down the hills.

A mixup in titles and surveys and court orders and one thing and another came to a head at the ranch of a man named Smith, who managed to prove his claim to the land, then sold a right-of-way to Harriman. As there was no other route to Bend from this point, other than over the Smith place, Hill decided to arbitrate matters, and a truce was made by which Hill agreed to build no further than Bend and to permit Harriman to use his line on which to run Harriman trains from Metolius, 42 miles from Bend. Three pictures portray the area where the Hill-Harriman war was waged in the Deschutes Canyon. One shows a road on the west bank where tracks were once laid by the Deschutes Railroad.

Scenes from the Deschutes Canyon,
where the Hill-Harriman war was waged.

James J. Andrews and William A. Fuller, principals in the actual "Great Locomotive Chase."

Pursuant to Walt Disney productions, only the signs had to be changed at stations of the Tallulah Falls Railway, e.g., from Lakemont to Etowah. The locomotive in the picture is the William Mason, 1856, named in honor of William Mason of Taunton, Mass., often referred to as "The Father of the American Type of Engine."

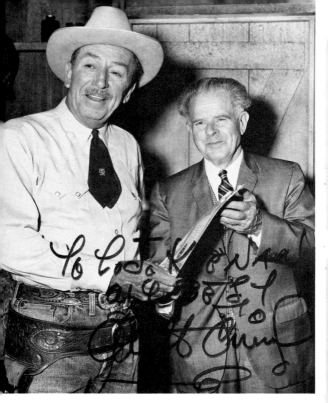

Above: Jeff Keenan presents Certificate of Award to Walt Disney in person in Studio One at Burbank, California, July 22, 1964. Disney autographed the picture in gratitude for their long friendship.

SANTA FE & DISNEYLAND R. R.

THE SCENIC ROUTE AROUND DISNEYLAND VIA THE
SPECTACULAR GRAND CANYON . . . and A JOURNEY
INTO THE FANTASTIC PRIMEVAL WORLD

This is to certify that

C. J. Keenan

IS AN HONORARY VICE-PRESIDENT OF
THE SANTA FE & DISNEYLAND RAILROAD

No. 018 _____ PRESIDENT

VOID AFTER DATE 1967

WALT DISNEY

December 30, 1966

Dear Mr. Keenan -

Walt always took great pleasure in renewing the title of Honorary Vice President on the Santa Fe & Disneyland Railroad to a small number of his friends and associates.

Prior to going into the hospital he went over the list for the coming year and approved a number of the passes, including yours.

While he did not have a chance to sign it I know he would want you to have the pass and the enjoyment it brings.

Sincerely,

Tommie Wilck

Secretary to Walt Disney

Mr. C. J. Keenan
National Railroad Hall of Fame & Museum
2545 S. W. Terwilliger Boulevard
Portland 1, Oregon

TW:lh
Enclosure

Right: The letter from Tommie is self-explanatory. Regarding the Disneyland Pass No. 018 above, the author trusts he can take it with him to the Great Beyond, where hopefully it will be signed.

Left: Sir William Cornelius Van Horne, J. C. M. G., was imbued with superhuman energy. He was once described as "a dynamo, run by dynamite." No one dared suggest to him that something was impossible; he delighted in impossibilities. He bore down on his problems like a locomotive at full steam, blowing a warning whistle, maybe, but still coming on fast, without applying brakes.

Right: William Henry Osborn entered the service of the Illinois Central Railroad unobtrusively, and apparently without an official title. But before many months had passed he had become a power in the affairs of the company. Though he had never been engaged in the railway business, he mastered the details with astonishing facility and soon demonstrated that he was an able executive of mature judgment and sound views in financial matters, and possessed an uncanny gift for judging men.

Left: Presenting the Certificate of Award to The Filson Club of Louisville in 1962 is J. C. Grisson, then vice president of the Louisville & Nashville Railroad, now retired. Accepting for The Filson Club is Richard H. Hill. At that time he was secretary of the Club. The large portrait in the background is an oil painting of Mr. Fink, also presented to The Filson Club by the L&N.

Right: Even in the colorful and adventurous history of American railroad development, where great individual achievements have been a common pattern, the accomplishments of Isaac Burton Tigrett were extraordinary. His is the sage of the true builder whose creative efforts contributed infinitely more to life than he took from it.

The Wedding of the Rails

C. J. KEENAN

PORTLAND, OREGON

GOLDEN SPIKE
CENTENNIAL CELEBRATION COMMISSION

HONORS BANQUET

SATURDAY, MAY 10, 1969 • 8:30 P.M.

LAFAYETTE BALLROOM - HOTEL UTAH

SALT LAKE CITY, UTAH

ADMIT ONE

No. One

Union Pacific Rail Road

GOLDEN SPIKE CENTENNIAL CELEBRATION

GOOD FOR ONE PASSAGE SALT LAKE CITY TO OGDEN and RETURN MAY 10, 1969 ONLY

Name Jeff Keenan

Car #: One

Chairman of Board

Title National Railroad of Fame

President

GOLDEN SPIKE CENTENNIAL CELEBRATION

Top left: The Wedding of the Rails. Lower left: Centennial Banquet at Lafayette Ballroom, Hotel Utah, Salt Lake City, Utah. Top right: Union Pacific Rail Road Pass No. 1 presented to Jeff for his passage, Salt Lake City to Ogden and return.

1869   1970

101st ANNIVERSARY

GOLDEN SPIKE CELEBRATION

MAY 9, 11:00 A.M.

GOLDEN SPIKE NATIONAL HISTORIC SITE

Above: Golden Spike Ceremony, 101st Anniversary program at Golden Spike Historic Site, May 10, 1970.

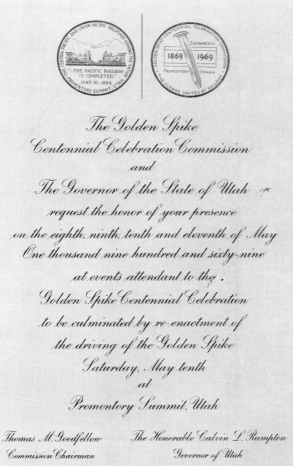

The Golden Spike
Centennial Celebration Commission
and
The Governor of the State of Utah
request the honor of your presence
on the eighth, ninth, tenth and eleventh of May
One thousand nine hundred and sixty-nine
at events attendant to the
Golden Spike Centennial Celebration
to be culminated by re-enactment of
the driving of the Golden Spike
Saturday, May tenth
at
Promontory Summit, Utah

Thomas M. Goodfellow
Commission Chairman

The Honorable Calvin L. Rampton
Governor of Utah

Reservation card enclosed

Right: Invitation to The Golden Spike Centennial Celebration at Promontory Summit, May 10, 1969.

Left: Theodore Dehone Judah, who interested the "Big Four" merchants of Sacramento—Leland Stanford, Collis P. Huntington, Mark Hopkins and Charles Crocker—in the idea of building a railroad eastward over the Sierra Nevada Mountains, was also instrumental in getting favorable consideration in Congress for the railroad project. He died, November 2, 1863, at the age of thirty-seven, ten months after ground for the building of the railroad had been broken at Sacramento.

Right: The first successful emergency stop in railroad history occurred unexpectedly in April 1869. George Westinghouse, twenty-three years old then, had made his first air brake and had persuaded the Panhandle Railroad to arrange a test run. As the train emerged from a tunnel, the engineer saw a huckster's cart on the tracks two blocks away and, "without much faith," reached for the strange brake handle. The brakes took hold and the locomotive stopped four feet from the cart. There could have been no more dramatic test had it been planned. The railroad officials on the train had just witnessed the first practical application of the Westinghouse air brake, an invention which has justly been called the "most important safety device ever known."

Left: Peter Cooper managed to combine innate intelligence, personal drive, and a broad social consciousness in a productive career that was dedicated to the public good. His 92-year lifetime was a success story that might have inspired the pen of a Horatio Alger.

Right: Henry Huttleston Rogers, who had an outstanding role in the building of The Virginian Railway.

HORATIO ALLEN as of July 4, 1958. Certificate of Award reposes in the Official Library of the Southern Railway at Washington, D.C. Employed by the Delaware & Hudson Canal Company, unaided and alone, he drove the "Stourbridge Lion" on its history-making run of about three miles from Honesdale to Seeleyville, Pa., and return on August 8, 1829. His recommendation in 1829 to adopt steam locomotives as the motive power for the South Carolina Canal and Rail Road was, as he wrote later, based "On the broad ground that there was no reason to expect any material improvement in the breed of horses, while in my judgment the man was not living who knew the breed of locomotives was to place at command." The South Carolina Canal and Rail Road became a part of the Southern Railway System.

JOHN WORK GARRETT as of July 4, 1958. Certificate of Award reposes in the Baltimore & Ohio Museum at Baltimore. Although Southern-born, he dedicated his own services and those of the railroad, which served as the life line of the North, to the Union cause. He was President Lincoln's principal advisor on transportation during the Civil War. The first military rail-transport movement in history, that of the transfer of 20,000 men and supplies from the Potomac to Chattanooga in 1863, was a monumental triumph for him and early railroad management.

GRENVILLE MELLEN DODGE as of July 4, 1959. Certificate of Award reposes in the Union Pacific Railroad Historical Museum at Omaha, Nebraska. Surveys and reconnaissance for the Union Pacific Railroad, 1853-60. It was upon this reconnaissance that Congress based its authorization for the construction of a Pacific Railroad in 1862. Upon completion of the first transcontinental railroad with the driving of the golden spike at Promontory Point, Utah, on May 10, 1869, he accomplished the greatest ambition of his life.

JAMES JEROME HILL as of July 4, 1959. Certificate of Award reposes in the Great Northern Railway Museum at St. Paul, Minnesota. Died May 29, 1916, in St. Paul, Minnesota, when transformation of the last American frontier—the vast, fertile Northwest country—into a rich, productive empire was at the zenith. And, on it, the man known the world around as the "Empire Builder" left his own monument—the Great Northern Railway.

CYRUS K. HOLLIDAY as of July 4, 1959. Certificate of Award reposes in the Santa Fe Railway Museum at Chicago, Illinois. People gathered in Topeka, Kansas, on October 30, 1868, to witness the first act in the construction of the Santa Fe Railroad. Yet, in reality, it was not the physical act of construction which brought these people together. Rather it was the result of the activities of a man able to use his opportunities. That man was Cyrus K. Holliday, founder and first president of the Santa Fe Railway, and the founder of Topeka, Kansas.

THEODORE DEHONE JUDAH as of July 4, 1959. Certificate of Award reposes in the Southern Pacific Lines Museum at San Francisco, California. At the age of twenty-eight he became Chief Engineer of the Sacramento Valley Railroad, the first steam-operated railroad west of the Rocky Mountains, and oldest portion of Southern Pacific's Western lines. Called by many skeptics of his day "Crazy Judah" because of his deep obsession to have a part in building the nation's first transcontinental railroad, in 1860, he surveyed a route across the Sierra Nevada Mountains through Donner Pass. The joining of East and West by railroad at Promontory Point, Utah, on May 10, 1869, was marked by the famed "Last Spike" ceremony, but Theodore Dehone Judah did not live to see this lifelong dream of his fulfilled.

GEORGE WESTINGHOUSE as of July 4, 1959. Certificate of Award reposes in Westinghouse Museum at Pittsburgh, Pennsylvania. Natural talent is God-given. It can be used selfishly for self-enrichment, or constructively, by directing its benefits toward advancement of the social order. George Westinghouse chose the latter course. He was not merely a great inventor and engineer, he was an industrialist in the broadest sense. He had the faculty for dealing with men and organizing them for research, development and manufacturing—a rare combination.

PETER COOPER as of July 4, 1960. Certificate of Award reposes in The Cooper Union, Cooper Square, in New York City. When Peter Cooper died, the City of New York went into mourning to pay tribute to a man who had been called "the first citizen of New York." His inventive genius was always at work, and in 1829 he built the "Tom Thumb" for the Baltimore and Ohio Railroad, the first successful locomotive to be used in America.

COLLIS POTTER HUNTINGTON as of July 4, 1960. Certificate of Award reposes in the Chesapeake and Ohio Railway Museum at Huntington, West Virginia. He was one of the four Sacramento merchants, the others being Charles Crocker, Mark Hopkins, and Leland Stanford, who were to be known as "the Big Four," and they were to become famous as the men who built the Central Pacific Railroad. However, it was Theodore Dehone Judah, civil engineer, who conceived the idea of building the Pacific Railroad, and after failing to interest San Francisco financiers, got the backing of the four Sacramento merchants, whom he started towards becoming the greatest railroad builders of the time. Collis Potter Huntington was the foremost builder of the Chesapeake and Ohio Railway. Many times I was enthralled by C. & O. trains passing through Deepwater as I was thrilled holding the hands of Sally Morgan while sitting on the banks of the Kanawha River. It was always a sight to watch C. & O. trains go by, especially the Fast Flying Virginian with Uncle Billy Richardson at the throttle with his long white beard fluttering out the cab window. Many businessmen in the financial district considered Collis Potter Huntington the "Abou Ben Adhem" of the railroad industry—a builder, not a manipulator of railroad stocks.

FREDERICK J. KIMBALL as of July 4, 1960. Certificate of Award reposes in the Norfolk and Western Railway Museum at Roanoke, Virginia. He joined the Norfolk and Western Railway the day it was reorganized from the ailing Atlantic, Mississippi and Ohio Railroad in 1881. He made an extreme study in Virginia geology. He studied reports of southwest Virginia coal deposits dating to the first explorations around 1750, and found mention of a rich coal outcropping in an 1870 paper describing Abbs Valley in the remote mountains southwest of New River. So, in May 1881, he led a party to the area and dug and tested the first coal from the rich Pocahontas seam, remarking "This may be the most important day in our lives."

WALTER McQUEEN as of July 4, 1960. Certificate of Award reposes in ALCO Products (Formerly American Locomotive Works, Schenectady plant) Museum at Schenectady, New York. Under his direction the Schenectady plant built good, reliable engines that were speedy and economical to operate. They were often affectionately referred to as the "McQueens." Even old Number 999 of endless fame had all the earmarks of the McQueen locomotives, although it was built by the New York Central & Hudson River Railroad at their West Albany shops the year Walter McQueen died.

HENRY HUTTLESTON ROGERS as of July 4, 1960. Certificate of Award reposes with descendants of William Rogers Coe, his grandson. He discovered NAPHTHA and became closely associated with John D. Rockefeller. However, his life must have been devoted more towards railroads as proved by the outstanding role in the building of The Virginian Railway.

SIR WILLIAM CORNELIUS VAN HORNE, K.C.M.G. as of January 1, 1961. Certificate of Award reposes in Windsor Station, Canadian Pacific Railway at Montreal, Canada. Born in Will County, Illinois, he started his eminent railroad career as a telegraph boy for the Illinois Central Railroad at Chicago. Step by step he rose from there until at the age of twenty-six he became Superintendent of the Chicago and Alton Railroad. After serving with that and other railroads, and gaining recognition through the vitality his methods breathed into various dying railroads, he became General Superintendent of the Chicago, Milwaukee and St. Paul Railroad, in 1879. On New Year's Day of 1882, he took over at Winnipeg as General Manager of the Canadian Pacific Railway to embark on the phenomenal construction which pushed through the line over the Rock Mountain barrier which Captain Palliser, the English explorer, had called impenetrable and was forced to yield before this human dynamo.

WILLIAM HENRY OSBORN as of February 10, 1961. Certificate of Award reposes in official library of Illinois Central Railroad at Chicago, Illinois. Among the outstanding men who directed the affairs of the company in its formative years, none deserves a higher place. He was a commanding figure in the affairs of the com-

Edward H. Harriman (left) and Leland Stanford—two key figures in the Railroad System, who were enshrined during the historic ceremonies at Ogden's Union Station, August 16, 1969. Leland Stanford, a former governor of California and one-time Central Pacific official during the driving of the Golden Spike in 1869, and E. H. Harriman, past president of the Union Pacific and one of the most significant figures of the century, became the 20th and 21st members of the Railroad Hall of Fame. As Chairman of the Board, I presented Certificates of Award honoring both men. Among the distinguished speakers at the ceremonies were Governor Calfin L. Hampton; United States Senator Wallace F. Bennett, R-Utah; United States Senator Frank Moss, D-Utah; and U.S. Representative Laurence J. Burton, R-Utah.

Local dignitaries included Ogden Mayor Bart Wolthuis, Brigham City Mayor Olef E. Zundel, and others. Railroad officials from both Union Pacific and Southern Pacific also were on hand for the ceremonies. Nathan H. Mazer, field director for the National Golden Spike Centennial Celebration Commission, termed the ceremony "an historic occasion." He added, "It is appropriate that the Ogden Union Station be the facility for the program."

Jeff presenting Certificate of Award to Mr. Bowra. Looking on are John Gzowski, a grandson of Sir Casimir with his wife and daughter from Dunnville, Ontario. Sir Casimir Stanislaus Gzowski was born, March 8, 1813, in St. Petersburg (now Leningrad), Russia. Son of a Polish nobleman, he was exiled to the United States in 1833 for his part in the Warsaw Rebellion against Russia. In 1838 he became a lawyer and a U.S. citizen. He married Maria Beebe, daughter of an eminent Philadelphia physician the next year. During 1841 he settled in Toronto, and became a naturalized citizen in 1846.

Quoting the June 9, 1963, issue of the *Buffalo Courier-Express*: "The man who engineered the 90-year-old International Bridge between Black Rock and Fort Erie was enshrined in the National Railroad Hall of Fame Saturday in a ceremony near the center of the span. Sir Casimir, who died in 1898, was engineer of a number of railroad projects including the bridge, 1870-1873.

"A Shrine certificate was presented by Jeff Keenan, Chairman of the Board of the Hall of Fame, Portland, Oregon, to W. C. Bowra, general manager of the Great Lakes Region of the Canadian National Railways. Fifty persons viewed the event on a special flat car that had been pushed out on the bridge and stopped at the International boundary on its way to Black Rock."

A group picture of notables, including C. P. Brzozowwicz, President, Association of Polish Engineers in Canada, fourth from right.

International Steam Bridge ferry that transported railroad cars, other vehicles, and people, prior to completion of the bridge.

pany from 1854 to 1883, a period of thirty years. He was president of the company from 1855 to 1865, years which included the Panic of 1857 and the Civil War, a most critical period in the railroad's history. Upon his shoulders, more than upon those of any other man of that period, fell the responsibility of steering the railroad through some of its most difficult times and of setting its course for the future.

ALBERT FINK as of April 3, 1962. Certificate of Award reposes in the Filson Club of Louisville, Kentucky. He was a giant in intellectual accomplishments as well as physical stature—he was six feet seven—and a man of three careers: he was an inventive engineer, an effective railroad executive and economist, and a far-seeing railroad statesman. These careers were sequential and, to some extent, concurrent, as one led into another. Largely because of his operational and executive skills, the Louisville and Nashville Railroad at the end of the Civil War was one of the few Southern railroads not bankrupt, or on the verge of bankruptcy.

ISAAC BURTON TIGRETT as of April 20, 1962. Certificate of Award reposes in the Gulf, Mobile and Ohio (now part of the Illinois Central Gulf) Museum at Mobile, Alabama. It was his creative alchemy which transferred bankrupt railroads into a prosperous system. The growth of the Gulf, Mobile and Ohio Railroad and the enviable position it occupied in the transportation industry attest to Mr. Tigrett's financial and administrative acumen. During a period of severe winter weather in a depression year, he instructed agents to keep stations open day and night to provide comfort for all persons seeking shelter. Each of the chapters of his book of life was a fascinating record of a task well done, whether in the field of railroad management or of some cultural or humanitarian undertaking.

SIR CASIMIR STANISLAUS GZOWSKI as of June 8, 1963. Certificate of Award reposes in the Central Station of Canadian National Railways at Montreal, Quebec, Canada. As an engineer and educator he took a very active interest in Canada's development from the start until his death. He engineered the construction of the International Bridge across the Niagara River, linking Bridgeburg (now Fort Erie) with Buffalo (1870-1873), considered to be one of the most

gigantic engineering works on the North American continent up to that time. He engineered the construction of the Great Western Railroad, now Canadian National. Among his other engineering feats was the widening of the Welland Canal allowing ocean-going ships to pass through.

EDWARD HENRY HARRIMAN as of August 16, 1969. Certificate of Award presented to D.F. Wengart, Assistant Chief Executive Officer of the Union Pacific Railroad, on behalf of the Harriman family. During the panic of 1893, the Union Pacific paid heavily for its previous overexpansion and bad financing. The property was sold at foreclosure, November 1, 1897, to the present Union Pacific Railroad Company. Soon after this new company was launched, Edward Henry Harriman emerged as the dominant figure in its management. He put the railroad on a solid foundation and started it on the road to what it is today, one of the outstanding railroads in the world.

LELAND STANFORD as of August 16, 1969. Certificate of Award presented to his grandnephew Leland Stanford. At the beginning of construction, the Central Pacific was referred to as "Stanford's moonshine project" and newspapers freely predicted that there would never be a railroad to Nevada by the way of Dutch Flat, for the obstacles were too great. Because he was the most commanding figure in the public eye in his little group of railroad builders, Stanford shoveled the first earth when work started on the Central Pacific Railroad, January 8, 1863, and he was called upon to drive the last spike six years later, May 10, 1869, when the Central Pacific tracks met those of the Union Pacific at Promontory, Utah.

SIR DONALD ALEXANDER SMITH as of November 4, 1970. Certificate of Award presented to J.N. Fraine, Senior Regional Vice President of the Canadian Pacific Railway, in his office of the CPR station at Vancouver, British Columbia. Always interested in railroads, he realized the Canadian West needed immigrants to fulfill a great potential. British Columbia had agreed to enter the Confederation on promise that a railway would be built and Sir Donald, although not officially a member of the 1880 syndicate formed to build the line, risked his personal fortune to keep the venture afloat. The honor and recognition of his persistence came with an invitation to drive the last spike in 1885, the year before he was knighted by Queen Victoria.

ENSHRINEMENTS—
HALL OF ROMANCE

Nine persons honored starting with Jonathan Luther (Casey) Jones, continuing on to Walter Elias (Walt) Disney.

Persons enshrined in the Hall of Romance are as follows:

JONATHAN LUTHER (CASEY) JONES as of April 30, 1961. For more than a century the steam locomotive was supreme in railroad service—and it was on such an engine that Casey Jones rode to his death and to his immortal fame as the symbol of the devotion to duty which caused him to stick by his engine when he was faced, suddenly, with death as his train plunged into the cars of a freight train fouling the main track on the morning of April 30, 1900, at Vaughan, Mississippi.

JANIE (MRS. CASEY) JONES as of April 30, 1961. Certificate of Award reposes in the Casey Jones Museum at Jackson, Tennessee. When Casey was killed at Vaughan, Mississippi, he had just recently been transferred to Memphis on Illinois Central's crack passenger train, the "Cannonball Express." Mrs. Jones was still living in Jackson, Tennessee, when the news came. She reared and educated her three children all alone, having never married again. In tribute to his memory she dressed in black every day in the fifty-eight years she lived after Casey's death. As time passed she became somewhat of a celebrity. Frequently over the years she was feted at various events such as the World's Fair in New York City in 1939.

SIMEON T. (SIM) WEBB as of April 30, 1961. Certificate of Award reposes in the Casey Jones Museum at Jackson, Tennessee. First employed by the Illinois Central Railroad as a call boy at McComb, Mississippi, in about 1893. Three years later he was promoted to locomotive fireman. In 1899 he became Casey Jones's fireman. When Casey was transferred to passenger service he was accompanied by Sim. Coming into Memphis the night of April 29, 1900, Casey and Sim stepped down from the cab into an emergency situation. The engineer who was to take the "Cannon Ball Express" on the run to Canton, Mississippi, was ill. Casey was asked to double back although he had time for only a short rest. He agreed, provided he could have Sim as his fireman. Roaring down the track at a terrific speed, Casey soon made up most of the hour and a half they were behind leaving Memphis, as he neared Vaughan, Mississippi. Rounding the curve above the switch, Casey saw the rear end of a freight train fouling the main track. He set the air brakes but it was too late. "Better jump" he shouted to Sim and Sim did. The doughty fireman survived the most famous train wreck of American history.

ROBERT TAYLOR (BOB) McMILLAN as of October 1, 1960. Certificate of Award reposes in the museum of the Centralia Historical Society, Centralia, Illinois. He became a locomotive fireman in 1894. He was promoted to engineer on August 13, 1899. When he swung down from the lead cab unit on the City of New Orleans on February 8, 1956, at the age of eighty-three, he was the oldest locomotive engineer in the United States and he was winding up a career of sixty-seven years with the Illinois Central Railroad. The first engine he ever ran did not have a cab nor seat box because she had been side-swiped that morning. A railing was put up around the side to keep the engineer and fireman from falling off. The only protection from the weather was an old umbrella which was soon torn to shreds. However, he made the trip successfully so earned his spurs as an engineer. For having achieved a unique record in the field of railroading by reason of his unequaled and skillful service which captured national recognition, the citizens of Centralia, Illinois, set up a monument in his honor, which was dedicated on October 1, 1960.

KATHERINE CARROLL (KATE) SHELLEY as of July 6, 1961. Certificate of Award reposes in the Iowa State Historical Museum at Des Moines, Iowa. In 1866, the Shelley family came to the United States and settled near Moingona, Iowa. Her father was employed as a section foreman by the Chicago and Northwestern

Left: Artist's drawing of Kate Shelley making her perilous way on hands and knees across the long Des Moines bridge.

R. T. (Bob) McMillan, still a "Hogger" (locomotive engineer) at eighty-two. This picture was taken at Cairo, Illinois, May 1955. "Polecat" McMillan received his nickname from an encounter with a skunk at the time he was a locomotive fireman for the Illinois Central Railroad. Bob told the author about the time when he and his "intended" were driving along a country road in a horse and buggy one night and the oil lights on each side of the buggy barely showed what appeared to be a cat in the center of the road. The lady had him stop the buggy and asked that he remove the "cat" so they would not run over it. Bob got within a short distance of the "cat" but then walked home.

"Polecat" was fond of saying the railroad had paid him for doing the one thing he wanted to do more than anything else in the world—drive a locomotive.

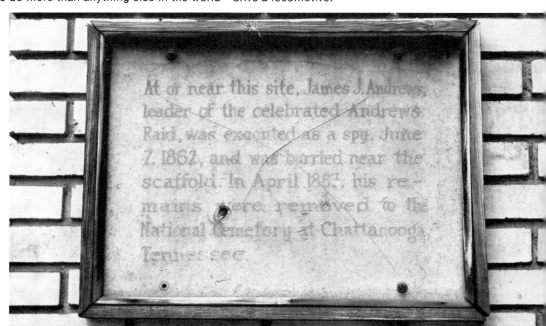

Plaque of James J. Andrews at S.E. Juniper Street and 3rd Avenue, Atlanta, Georgia.

One of the last pictures taken of Jesus Garcia, who saved the city of Nacozari from destruction and became one of the railroad heroes of all time.

Author's presentation of Certificate of Award honoring Jesus Garcia to President Adolpho Mateos on November 7, 1963, in the National Palace at Mexico City.

Railway at the time of his death on December 1, 1879. Torrential rains for a week had brought to flood stage all streams in the area, followed by a cloudburst the night of July 6, 1881. Before the next morning her mother learned how her daughter, Kate, saved the lives of several hundred persons in spite of the storm. In weeks to come, so did the rest of the United States. The railroad had sent out a pilot engine to test the track. Through a flash of lightning, Kate saw the locomotive drop through a break in the bridge into the churning waters of Honey Creek. With the Chicago and Northwestern Railway Atlantic Express due in an hour, Kate, only fifteen at the time, went out into the darkness and the storm. She made her perilous way on hands and knees across the long Des Moines River bridge and finally bleeding and exhausted, to Moingona Station just in time to warn of the danger and avert disaster.

CAPTAIN WILLIAM ALLEN FULLER as of April 12, 1962. Certificate of Award presented to his daughter-in-law, Mrs. Margaret L. Fuller, at her home in Atlanta, Georgia. The Andrews Raiders failed from causes which reflected neither upon the genius of their plan nor upon the intrepidity and discretion of those in conducting it. But for the marvelous nerve and physical endurance of the Confederate pursuers, led by Captain Fuller, the movement would have been a complete success, and the whole aspect of the war in the South would have been at once changed. Much to the amusement of people present that morning, Captain Fuller started out on foot from Big Shanty, Georgia. Two miles down the track he secured a section car and pushed it back to Big Shanty. Picking up his engineer and master mechanic, they pushed and rode it to Etowah, where they took over the "Yonah," the first of three locomotives used in the pursuit. The chase ended nineteen miles south of Chattanooga, where the "Texas" caught up with the "General" that had run out of fuel.

JAMES J. ANDREWS as of June 10, 1963. Certificate of Award reposes in the Ohio State Museum at Columbus, Ohio. There were few more romantic figures among those who rose into prominence during the great Civil War than James J. Andrews. On April 12, 1862, the greatest locomotive chase in all history took place. Early that morning, the regular Western and Atlantic Railroad passenger train left Atlanta for Chattanooga, with Captain Fuller in charge as conductor. The Andrews Raiders, under the leadership of James J. Andrews, boarded the train at Marietta, Georgia. They seized the historic war locomotive, the "General," and two box cars at Big Shanty, Georgia, and rode northward for the purpose of burning the bridges on that line, thereby dismembering the Confederacy. James Andrews and most of his men were captured, and on June 7, 1862, in Atlanta, he was the first to be strung up for stealing the locomotive. He was jerked right into glory and history with a rope so faulty they had to dig under the unconscious man to get enough air for him to dance on.

JESUS GARCIA as of November 7, 1963. The Certificate of Award was presented to his Excellency, Adolpho Mateos, President of the Mexican Republic, in the National Palace, Mexico, D.F. Garcia displayed early signs of his courage and quick-wittedness. In time he was promoted to engineer. One day as he was inching his locomotive and its consist of ore cars down a steep grade to El Porvenir, seven miles from Nacozari, the air brakes failed and his train began to run wild. It took all of the young engineer's ability to keep the train from plunging to destruction. That bit of expert railroading won for him the good will of James Douglas, president of the company, who afterward considered Garcia one of his friends. On November 7, 1907, Garcia was ordered down to the lower yard to bring back two cars carrying dynamite for the mine. The engine and two cars just reached the concentrating plant switch when he noticed that one of the cars was afire and called out to the train crew, who scattered when a single voice cried out: "Go away. . .leave me alone!" It was Garcia telling his men to seek safety for themselves. The town of Nacozari lay just in front of the train. Garcia pulled away with the dynamite and raced for the hillside. Had the explosion been nearer the town, Nacozari would have been erased from the face of the earth. Jesus Garcia had sacrificed his own life to save the people of Nacozari.

WALT DISNEY (Walter Elias Disney) as of July 22, 1964. Certificate of Award presented to Walt in Studio One at Burbank, California. If one thing was more amazing than the warm, wonderful, heart-stirring motion pictures of

Walt Disney, it was the man who made them. Walt's romance with railroads began as a teenage trainboy selling newspapers and confectionery on Santa Fe trains between Chicago and Kansas City. There are some people who suspect that Walt built the park's mile and a half long Santa Fe and Disneyland Railroad as the outgrowth of his lifelong love of trains. The now abandoned Tallulah Falls Railway, formerly in operation between Cornelia, Georgia, and Franklin, North Carolina, was made to order for Walt's production, "The Great Locomotive Chase." Station buildings needed only the change in signs to correspond with names of places on the old Western and Atlantic Railroad between Big Shanty and Ringgold, Georgia, the route of the greatest locomotive chase in history.

THOMAS ALVA EDISON

From trainboy to one of the greatest industrial geniuses of the United States. . .published the only newspaper ever regularly printed on a moving train . . .built the first successful electric railway in the world.

It was once said by one of the greatest industrial geniuses of the United States that "We are ahead of all other countries today, simply and solely because we have Thomas Alva Edison." The Edison family moved to Port Huron, Michigan, in 1854. Thomas Alva Edison became a trainboy at the age of twelve. While serving in this capacity he set up a small hand press in a corner of the baggage car. With this equipment he published the *Grand Trunk Herald*. This little weekly was one of the few if not the only newspaper ever regularly printed on a moving train. The future inventor also was carrying on chemical experiments. One day some of the chemicals were spilled and set fire to the baggage car. The train conductor put the young fellow and all his paraphernalia out of the baggage car and this ended the career of the newspaper.

One day, the infant son of the station agent at Mt. Clemens, Michigan, strayed onto the tracks. Young Edison saw that the child was in the path of an oncoming train. Without a moment to spare, he leaped forward, seized the child and was just able to throw himself and the

little boy out of the way. In gratitude for this, the father taught Edison the art of sending and receiving telegraph messages. Edison soon became a rapid and accurate operator.

Thomas A. Edison built the first successful electric railway in the world at Menlo Park, New Jersey, in 1880. Electricity was first successfully applied to street-railway operation in 1888, and within a few years practically all of the street railways had adopted electricity, wholly or in part, as motive power. Construction of interurban systems began in 1897.

The operation of interurban electric railways presented an entirely different problem. While such lines were largely the extension of city lines, in many cases they became distinct transportation units, considered with the view of serving outlying territory—and in some cases connecting the larger cities. Chiefly passenger-carrying railways at first, no freight was handled, but soon they commenced handling what is ordinarily termed "package freight" on their passenger cars—more in the nature of express business than freight business. Gradually the freight business increased until after several years some of the roads began the operation of separate cars for freight.

The electric locomotive became a strong rival of the steam locomotive, which was gradually superseded by the diesel locomotive. On the Norfolk & Western Railway, coal trains of 3,250 tons were hauled up two percent grades by two electric locomotives at double the speed formerly attained by three of the largest Mallet steam locomotives. The great power of the electric hauler is due to the fact that a much larger percentage of its total weight can be developed to the apparatus that rotates its wheels, as it carries no heavy boiler but draws its energy from an outside source, the power-house. For several years, railroads have relied mostly on diesel power for operation of trains, thus discontinuing the use of power energy on some lines.

The comparative economy of diesel and electric locomotives for railway service is still under discussion, but it is generally conceded by mechanical engineers that electric traction is to be preferred (1) in tunnel operation, (2) in large cities and their suburbs, (3) where sufficient water power is available, and (4) where superplants can be built near to an adequate supply of low-grade combustible coal for use as the initial fuel of such power plants.

Edison Electric Railway, 1880.

Left: the first railroad employment of Casey Jones was that of brakeman for the Mobile and Ohio Railroad in 1884. Casey, nicknamed after his hometown, Cayce, Kentucky, soon proved he was a natural-born railroad man. It was sometime during the year 1886 that Casey transferred his service to that of fireman for the Illinois Central Railroad. Less than three years later he was promoted to engineer. In 1898 he was assigned to passenger service. Right: Mrs. Martha Gilliam, curator, holding up Certificate of Award honoring Casey in the Casey Jones Museum at Jackson, Tennessee. Others in the picture are, left to right: Dewey Crocker, Chief Special Agent for the Gulf, Mobile & Ohio Railroad, at Jackson; Charles Jones, son of Casey, machinist for the Illinois Central; and Leroy Pope, attorney, an ardent worker in behalf of the Casey Jones Museum.

Simeon (Sim) Webb

Simeon (Sim) Webb (right) aboard the Louisville & Nashville Pan-American out of Memphis, Tennessee, on June 15, 1952, en route to Johnstown, Pa., for Railroad Day. This was under the auspices of the Casey Jones Railroad Unit of the American Topical Association, where Sim was honored as the third member of the Casey Jones Fellowship, better known as "The Big 4 of Railroad Romance." The picture was taken at Louisville, Ky., by Douglas C. Lanier, then city passenger agent for the L. & N. The picture at left was taken at Johnstown. The author accompanied Sim from Memphis to Johnstown, and then on to New York City, where he arranged for him to meet Jackie Robinson—his favorite baseball player—at the Polo Grounds.

One of the last pictures taken of Janie (Mrs. Casey) Jones on December 10, 1950, during Railroad Days at Buffalo, New York. She is standing between Bob Cornelius on the right and a friend of Bob's, both eminent businessmen who were instrumental in the celebration of Railroad Days. The Chesapeake & Ohio Railway prepared the mock locomotive cab for the picture. Janie Brady was scarcely out of pigtails when, about 1884, she first met Casey, a tall, handsome youth. He had recently arrived in Jackson to take a brakeman's job on the Mobile and Ohio Railroad. They soon fell in love and were married on November 29, 1886. She died on November 21, 1959, in Jackson, and now rests alongside Casey in Mt. Calvary Cemetery on the edge of Jackson—and nearby is a railroad. For many years engineers of "The Dixie Route" saluted Casey with two short blasts of the whistle. As long as trains pass by, the salute will be for Janie and Casey Jones.

The Ballad of Casey Jones

Wallace Saunders, negro wiper at the Illinois Central roundhouse, composed the words. Many vaudeville teams changed them slightly and made them their own by copyrighting them. The ballad has gone around the world. Casey Jones is known wherever there are railroads. Following is the original folk version:

Come, all you rounders, for I want you to hear
The story of a brave engineer;
Casey Jones was the rounder's name—
On a heavy six-wheeler he rode to fame.

Caller called Jones about half-past four,
Jones kissed his wife at the station door,
Climbed into the cab with orders in hand,
Says, "This is my trip to the promised land."

Through South Memphis yards on the fly,
He heard the fireman say, "You've got a white eye."
All the switchmen knew by the engine's moans
That the man at the throttle was Casey Jones.

It had been raining for more than a week,
The railroad track was like the bed of a creek.
They rated him down to a thirty-mile gate,
Threw the southbound mail about eight hours late.

Fireman says, "Casey, you're runnin' too fast—
You run the block signal the last station you passed."
Jones says, "Yes—think we can make it though,
For the steam's much better than ever I know."

Jones says, "Fireman, don't you fret,
Keep knocking' at the firedoor, don't give up yet;
I'm goin' to run her till she leaves the rail
Or make it on time with the south-bound mail."

Around the curve and a-down the dump
Two locomotives were a-bound to bump.
Fireman hollered, "Jones, it's just ahead,
We might jump and make it but we'll all be dead!"

'Twas around this curve he saw a passenger train;
Something happened in Casey's brain.
Fireman jumped off, but Casey stayed on—
He's a good engineer but he's dead and gone.

Poor Casey was always all right.
He stuck to his post both day and night.
They loved to hear the whistle of old Number Three
As he came into Memphis on the old K. C.

Headaches and heartaches and all kinds of pain
Are not apart from a railroad train;
Tales that are earnest, noble and gran'
Belong to the life of a railroad man.

THE BRAVE ENGINEER

"Stack talk" and its refrain. . .left arm on the throttle . . .time was important. . ."put her through on time" . . .plain greed and mismanagement a handicap. . . train of steam cars was magic.

Most engineers thought of their steam locomotives as if they were somewhat human, especially at night under the stars when the vast universe came to mind. "Stack talk" seemed to carry a refrain that only railroaders, especially engineers, could understand.

Many people will continue to think that a hero is a person honored after death by public worship, because of exceptional service to mankind. But what about the Brave Engineer, the man in the right-hand side of the locomotive cab, who drove his train safely through night and storm? He always looked ahead, scanning the bright rails for danger, his mind weighed with responsibility for his charges in the cars, his left arm resting on the throttle. It was his duty to put her through, or to die at his post, and die he too often did.

He was a great, magnificent figure to Young America. More than one banker and college president and eminent divine envied him, too, for his was the post they all had wanted and once meant to have, the calling for which superb whistles blew and noble bells rang, to the accompaniment of pounding drivers on the rails. He was the man who put her through, come what might of the weather or other elements.

Time was important to this man. Regardless of other employes, it was at last and finally the engineer who put her through on time.

The Brave Engineer and his iron horse had begun, even in the early days, to set the pace that was to hurry America to its material triumph. Pious men sought to stop its progress, on the first day of the week. Plain greed of speculators and mismanagement have been a handicap.

The railroads have usually been run by ingenious men, quick to sense a challenge of any sort, and quick to meet it. Of challenges and other dangers they have had their share. The Brave Engineer was one of the noblest Americans of them all, when a train of steam cars was magic that took one to all known places, and beyond. I find I bear this particular penalty of age very lightly. I even find room for pity of the generations too young to have known the steam railroad in its heyday, that lasted for some eighty years and cast a sorcery from which I, for one, have never attempted to escape. Let me sing of the magic steam cars of my day, and two generations before.

Lehigh Valley No. 681. Camelbacks kept firemen slim and hungry.

PART TWO

RAILWAY PHILATELY

Affinity between trains and postage stamps. . .railroad philatelists instrumental for issuance of cacheted covers honoring our great railroad and locomotive builders and persons memorable in railroad history . . .cacheted covers also issued commemorating important anniversaries of such trains as the 20th Century and Broadway Limiteds. . .organized the Casey Jones Railroad unit of the American Topical Association. . .blizzard mailman. . .Baltimore & Ohio Railroad's 125th birthday party. . .honors issued along the way. . .opening day of Disneyland, July 18, 1955 . . .Appointed president of American Topical Association. . .replacing rose tree on grave of Casey Jones at Jackson, Tennessee. . .ceremonies for the new Mid-Century Empire Builder and Western Star. . . exhibition by NARHFAM at the Oregon Centennial and International Trade Fair. . .ceremonies for inaugural runs of Portland Zoo Railway.

There is considerable affinity between trains and postage stamps. Quite apart from the fact that railroads are no longer chief carriers of first-class mail, there is another link which might at first be overlooked. The postage stamp and the railroad have, so to speak, grown up together, for each saw its public inception within a few years of the other. In this connection, there is a peculiar aspect. The Postoffice Department has never issued postal honors to our great railroad and locomotive builders, although they have commemorated about everything else, including a chicken. However, philatelists interested in railroads have been instrumental for the issuance of cacheted covers honoring our great railroad and locomotive builders and persons memorable in railroad history.

Postage stamps of topical design issued by various nations were part of the merchandise I sold on trains when I was a trainboy. A stamp issued by the Post Office Department commemorating the Pan American Exposition and depicting the Empire State Express glorified a train, but I became increasingly aware that nothing has ever been done in recognition of

Official cacheted cover commemorating 50th anniversary of the death of Casey Jones at Vaughan, Mississippi, April 30, 1900. This is the first-day issue of the postage stamp, April 29, 1950, honoring the Railroad Engineers of America, applied and autographed by Mrs. Casey Jones.

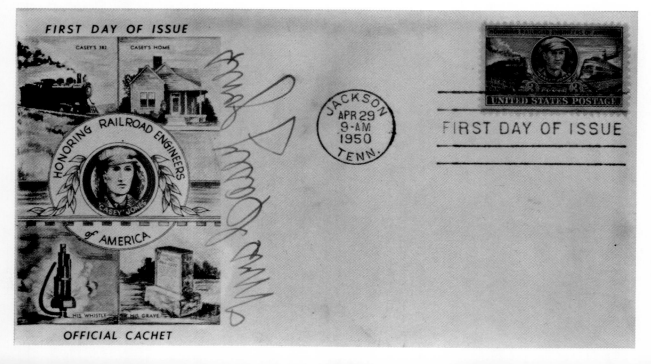

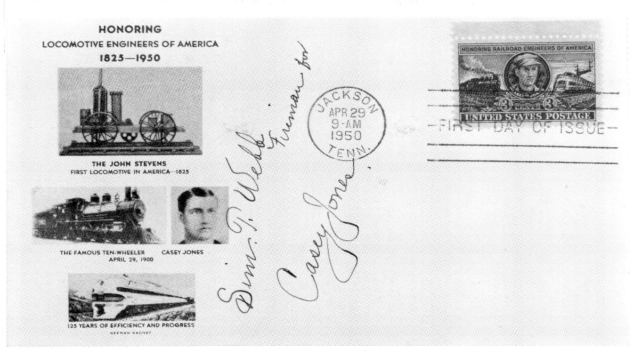

A Keenan-cacheted cover commemorating 50th anniversary of the death of Casey Jones at Vaughan, Mississippi, April 30, 1900. This is also the first-day issue of the postage stamp, April 29, 1950, honoring Railroad Engineers and autographed by Sim T. Webb, Casey Jones's fireman at the time of the accident.

persons for their achievements in railroad development. My awareness evolved with time. It took me a while, serving in various capacities on various railroads with their trials and tasks, to fully understand the eminence of their accomplishments and share in the job of conquest they felt in their satisfaction of performance. Since June 1, 1957, I have been able to give much more time to that part of our American heritage than ever before.

During November of 1949, I joined with Dewey Crocker, Division Special Agent of the former Gulf, Mobile & Ohio, the railroad on which Casey Jones started his notable career, and took a prominent part in having philatelic honors issued to commemorate the 50th anniversary of the death of Casey Jones. The first day of sale of the stamp was at Jackson, Tennessee, on April 29, 1950. Cacheted covers (envelopes bearing a post-office cancellation and date) were issued and also autographed by Mrs. Casey Jones and Sim Webb, Casey Jones's fireman, who survived the most famous train wreck of American history. During the ceremonies—with the blessing of Isaac Burton Tigrett, President of the Gulf, Mobile & Ohio Railroad and six other railroad presidents—the foundation was laid for establishing the Casey Jones Fellowship for conferring appropriate honors on not more than four living persons who had performed top roles in the romance of railroads. Mrs. Casey Jones, widow of the famous locomotive engineer, was the first person to receive that honor, followed by Sim Webb. The fellowship became better known as the "Big Four of Railroad Romance."

On February 3, 1951, I played the part of a "Blizzard Mailman" to fully service cacheted covers. The story was published in *Linn's Weekly Stamp News* as follows: "While stamp and cover collecting provides a bushel of fun all its own, adding to it now and again with a special stunt is like putting frosting on a delicious cake. Just recently I was engaged in applying some of the frosting to my philatelic cake —and I did it in zero weather during a blizzard.

"Some of the best skiing in the west is to be found on the slopes of Mount Hood in Oregon. The seeker of scenery will find a breathtaking panorama, winter or summer. Pursuers of both have been aided materially in their enjoyment by the construction of an aerial tramway which takes its passengers three miles up Mount Hood in moderate comfort. Name of this transportation is 'Skiway'. The cachet on the cover shows the cars suspended in the air on its cables near the lower terminal. The upper terminal is about 800 feet from Timberline Lodge.

"On February 3rd, Skiway began its first public service and I thought it would be an interesting stunt to prepare covers for the first

Carried on first upbound trip of SKIWAY COACHES from Government Camp to Timberline Lodge, Mt. Hood, Oregon, February 3, 1951.

SKIWAY, the world's largest and longest passenger-carrying aerial tramway, provides comfortable year-round tree-top level travel above evergreens and crags for three scenic miles up the slopes of Oregon's majestic Mt. Hood.

Carried on first downward trip of SKIWAY COACHES from Timberline Lodge to Government Camp, February 3, 1951.

SKIWAY, the world's largest and longest passenger-carrying aerial tramway, provides comfortable year-round tree-top level travel above evergreens and crags for three scenic miles up the slopes of Oregon's majestic Mt. Hood.

Cacheted covers commemorating the first upward and downward trips of Skiway Coaches.

upward trip of the tramway, and for the first downward trip. I carried the covers myself, both ways, a form of insurance on the success of the project hardly to be improved upon. The car arrived at the upper terminal without incident in its usual prosaic and routine manner. But to get a postmark on my covers, I had to travel the short distance to Timberline Lodge, where a post office is maintained, and 800 feet isn't much of a jaunt, even on a mountain.

"But that day was different. I stepped from the car into a raging blizzard in which visibility was absolutely zero. Since I knew the general direction to the Lodge rather well, I donned my skis, strapped on the packages of covers to my back and set out. I almost ran smack into the place before I knew I was there and almost stumbled over one of the St. Bernard dogs so familiar to folks who visit Mt. Hood.

"It might be of interest to note that Timberline Lodge was dedicated by the late President Franklin Roosevelt when he visited there in September 1937. It was this reason that on covers postmarked at Timberline Lodge I in-

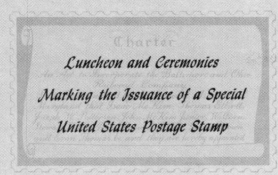

1827   1952

Luncheon and Ceremonies

Marking the Issuance of a Special

United States Postage Stamp

Commemorating

The One Hundred and Twenty-Fifth Anniversary

of the Granting of the Charter to

The Baltimore and Ohio Railroad Company

THE SHERATON BELVEDERE HOTEL

BALTIMORE, MARYLAND

Thursday, February 28, 1952

TWELVE O'CLOCK NOON

Program

➤➤➤ ⋘⋘⋘

Presiding...........................HOWARD E. SIMPSON
Vice President, Traffic, The Baltimore and Ohio Railroad Company

The National Anthem.........*Led by* JAMES ALLAN DASH
Conductor, Baltimore and Ohio Choral Clubs

Invocation.........*The Rt. Rev.* NOBLE C. POWELL, D.D.
Bishop of the Episcopal Diocese of Maryland

Address...............................MR. SIMPSON

Greeting............................NEAL A. SIBLEY
Postmaster of Baltimore

Presentation...........................C. J. KEENAN
President, The American Topical Association

Presentation Address..*The Honorable* OSBORNE A. PEARSON
Assistant Postmaster General of the United States

Acceptances:

The Honorable THEODORE R. MCKELDIN
Governor of Maryland

The Honorable THOMAS D'ALESANDRO, JR.
Mayor of Baltimore

The Honorable GEORGE L. RADCLIFFE
President of the Maryland Historical Society

MR. SIMPSON, FOR COLONEL R. B. WHITE
President, The Baltimore and Ohio Railroad Company

Program of luncheon and ceremonies marking the issuance of a special United States postage stamp.

cluded the 1 cent Roosevelt stamp and the 2 cent Lake Placid of 1932 that portrays a ski jumper.

"Downward trip covers were cancelled at Government Camp, Oregon, near the lower terminus of the tramway. This postmarking device too is of the hand-stamp variety. The post office stands on the old Oregon Trail used by many of the early settlers on their way to Western Oregon. The stamp portrays the Oregon Trail. My 'Operation Skiway' provided a lot of pleasure not the least of which was the opportunity of being able to add something unique to the albums of my friends."

I was an honored guest by special invitation of the president and directors of the Baltimore & Ohio Railroad at a luncheon February 28, 1952, at the Sheraton Belvedere Hotel, Baltimore, marking the 125th anniversary of the signing of its charter by the legislature of the State of Maryland and the issuance of a commemorative postage stamp by the U.S. Post Office Department—with first day of issue at Baltimore. Eminent speakers were Governor Theodore E. McKeldin, U.S. Senator Herbert R. O'Connor, Asst. Postmaster General Osborne A. Pearson, Thomas D'Alesandro, Mayor of Baltimore, and Howard E. Simpson for Colonel R.B. White, President of the B. & O. All members of the Maryland legislature attended the luncheon.

On my return trip from Baltimore to Portland, I stopped off at Chicago and discussed

Introduction of Jeff Keenan by Mr. H. E. Simpson, Vice President, Baltimore & Ohio Railroad: "Coming all the way from Portland, Oregon, is Mr. C. J. Keenan. He is President of an international stamp collectors' organization—The American Topical Association. He comes here to present to President White a gold membership card in the Casey Jones Railroad Unit of his society. Mr. Keenan, in Colonel White's absence, I will be glad to accept this for him."

servicing of cacheted covers commemorating the golden anniversary of the 20th Century Limited and the Broadway Limited with C.W. Reames, General Superintendent, Postal Transportation Service. We talked on the subject of R.P.O. (Railway Post Office) and station cancellation for ten thousand covers on June 15, 1952, the anniversary date. Mr. Reames suggested that I write to Honorable John W. Redding, Assistant Postmaster General at Washington, D.C. Mr. Redding's reply of March 31, 1952, to mine of March 15, 1952, follows: "Effort will be made to arrange for the handling of these covers at New York and Chicago at both of the rail stations used by these railroad companies. As soon as appropriate arrangements have been made and details obtained, I shall be pleased to advise you further concerning this matter."

Correspondence continued right up to just a few days before the anniversary date. All covers were proficiently serviced and Post Office Department officers and employes were kindly thanked for their efforts. Very few people who have received cacheted covers serviced under my supervision have had more than a vague supposition of the time and effort put forth for their consummation. The servicing of the "Broadway" and "Century" covers took weeks of planning, work, and many miles of travel— also much greater expense than I had anticipated. On the other hand, the letters received from several persons stating their emotions as to the beauty and integrity of the covers are of considerable satisfaction to me.

The inaugural runs of the new faster North Coast Limited and the Mainstreeter of the Northern Pacific Railway were commemorated on November 16, 1952, with special cacheted covers, and given extraordinary philatelic postage. During 1943-44, the U.S. Post Office Department issued a series of special stamps commemorating thirteen Overrun Countries, starting with Poland and ending with Korea. The flag stamp issued for Korea features the design called the Great Chinese Monad or Diagram of the Great Extreme.

At the Chicago World's Fair of 1893, E.H. McHenry, then Chief Engineer of the Northern Pacific, chanced to visit the Korean exhibit. Seeing the Korean flag, he was impressed by the simple but striking design it carried, because at that time the NP was searching for a suitable trademark, and Mr. McHenry realized almost immediately that this symbol could be adapted quite readily for that purpose. When he returned to St. Paul, he submitted his idea to Charles Fee, then General Passenger Agent, and together they worked out the emblem which became familiar to millions of Americans.

Curious about the origin of this symbol, Mr. McHenry began an investigation of its history. The information he sought was difficult to find, but from a number of sources—missionaries to China, students of the Orient and scholarly books of Oriental philosophy—a reasonably accurate history of the Monad was finally pieced together. For more than a half century, the Monad has served to identify the Northern Pacific Railway, until it became a component of the Burlington Northern System. But the emblem is more than just an attractive design; it is taken from a symbol nearly 1,000 years old, and the ideas this symbol represent date back at least 4,000 years before that. (These famous trains started out of Seattle and Chicago on their inaugural runs on November 16, 1952.)

The covers from Portland were carried on trains of the Spokane, Portland and Seattle Railway, from Portland to Spokane via Pasco, as indicated by the postmark, and clearing through the Transfer Office, R.M.S. (Railway Mail Service). All covers were affixed with stamps portraying the Korean flag depicting the Monad.

The first trip of Southern Pacific's Shasta Daylight was commemorated with a cacheted cover with appropriate postage. The Southern Pacific issued a beautiful souvenir brochure for the first trip, July 10, 1949. People were quite overwhelmed by the magnificence of this train, both the exterior and the interior.

Cacheted covers not only show the picture subject but also the name of the city and state, the date, and in some cases, the time of day and train number. Several of the more important covers are shown in this book because they are vital to railroad history. With few exceptions, I prepared and serviced them, including art work if needed for significance.

Railway Philately had its start when the railroads first began carrying U.S. Mail, May 17, 1847. The first U.S. postal car was placed in operation on the Hannibal & St. Joseph Railroad, July 28, 1862. The inaugural run of the Chicago, Burlington & Quincy Railroad fast mail was March 10, 1884, between Chicago and Council Bluffs, Omaha.

Years later the circled postmark on some mail indicated the names of famous trains, train numbers, direction of travel, ED for eastbound, WD for westbound, and letters R.P.O., as well as the date and time. This method was continued after the start of letters PTS for cancellation of postage. The circled postmark showing Grand Central Station Transfer Clerk used the letters RMS for cancellation of postage.

R.P.O. is the abbreviation for Railway Post Office, PTS for Postal Transportation Service, and RMS for Railway Mail Service. Special cacheted covers serviced for inaugural runs, anniversary trips, last-day runs, and for other special occasions were particularly valuable if their purpose was historical.

The American Topical Association was formed during September of 1949 for people interested in topical philately. I was appointed president by the Board of Directors as of September 16, 1950. As a charter member I was winner of the Grand Award of life membership, February 1, 1951, because of my acumen and efforts in behalf of the organization.

The late Jerry Everts of the *Buffalo Courier-Express*, in his column "As I See it,"—January 2, 1951 issue headed "Steam and Stamps"—wrote: "Jeff Keenan, field auditor for the Public Utilities Commission of Oregon, last September was elected president of the American Topical Association for his unceasing work for the association and his efforts to secure issuance of the Casey Jones memorial postage stamp."

The Jackson, Tennessee, *Sun*, in a January 1951 issue, noted: "A most impressive ceremony was conducted in the quiet graveyard in the outskirts of Jackson recently at the grave of John Luther 'Casey' Jones. These honors were sponsored by the Casey Jones Railroad Unit of the American Topical Association. This unit was formed but a few months ago, with Dewey Crocker, president, and Jeff Keenan, secretary. Both men are well known in philatelic and railroad circles as the ones who were active in promoting the issuance of the Casey Jones postage stamp.

"The first public activity was the replacing of the rose tree on the grave, since the one placed there by Jeff Keenan in behalf of the Brotherhood Locomotive Engineers, Oregon Division of the Union Pacific Railroad, last April, had been taken, perhaps as a souvenir or by vandals. As part of this ceremony a Life Membership in the new organization was bestowed upon Mrs. Casey Jones and upon President I.B. Tigrett of the Gulf, Mobile and Ohio Railroad, where Casey began his famous career. Dewey Crocker, President of the Unit, presented the gold membership cards."

On June 3, 1951, in behalf of the Casey Jones Railroad of A.T.A., I conducted the ceremonies for the new Mid-Century Empire Builder at the Portland Union Station before the inaugural run departed for Chicago. Ralph Wacther, the locomotive engineer, broke a bottle of champagne over the nose of the new train, while officials of the Spokane, Portland & Seattle and Great Northern railroads watched. I arranged for similar ceremonies of inaugural runs of the train, which were held in Seattle and Chicago. A similar formality was held at the Portland Union Station that evening for the new streamliner Western Star, replacing the old Oriental Limited. The Portland and Seattle sections of the new Mid-Century Empire Builder join at Spokane, where ceremonies were also held. Cacheted covers were issued to commemorate the inaugural runs of the new trains, Nos. 1, 2 and 4 posted thereon.

The forty-fifth anniversary of the entry by the Oregon Trunk Railway into Bend, Oregon, was commemorated with a beautiful cacheted cover, postmarked at Bend, September 2, 1956. The cover also commemorates the seventieth anniversary year that the first post office was established at Bend, and the twenty-fifth anniversary year of the Inside Gateway Route through California, Oregon and Washington, by the Western Pacific, Great Northern, and Spokane, Portland & Seattle railroads, which operated a special excursion train between Oakland, California, and Wishram, Washington, passing through Bend on September 2, 1956, and thence through the great gorge of the Deschutes River.

The golden anniversary of the Spokane, Portland & Seattle Railway was commemorated at Sheridan's Point, Washington, where the rails joined on March 11, 1908, with a cacheted cover issued March 11, 1958, carried on Train No. 6 and postmarked accordingly with an RMS cancellation.

NARHFAM exhibited at the Oregon Centennial and International Trade Fair from the opening day of June 10 to the closing day of September 17, 1959. Cacheted covers were issued starting with the first day saluting the Association of American Railroads, and the second day saluting the American Short Line Railroad Association. Thereafter a cacheted cover was issued each day saluting a different railroad in alphabetical order starting with the Aberdeen & Rockfish, the last being the Yreka Western on the closing day. Several railroads exhibited in NARHFAM's space. More would have participated if space had been available. The Portland Zoo Railway operated with steam power over its own tracks every day during the exposition.

"Certification of Initial Clearance" was issued by the Casey Jones Railroad Unit of the American Topical Association for the inaugural runs of the Portland Zoo Railway (Zoo Line) Trains Nos. 1 and 2 on June 9, 1958, signed by Mayor Terry Schrunk for the City of Portland, Bill Bisop as superintendent for the Zoo Line, and C.J. Keenan as secretary. The certificate carries a Casey Jones postage stamp and is postmarked

Portland, Oreg. Transfer Off., 8: A.M. Jun. 9, 1958.

The Portland Zoo Railway was the first recreational railroad to carry U.S. Mail, first day as of June 13, 1961. All letters mailed on Zoo Line trains are postmarked Portland Zoo Railway showing date of carriage, and specify "Official U.S. Railway Mail - Mailed on Portland Zoo Railway - Portland Zoological Gardens. Portland, Oregon. U.S.A."

Jerry Everts of the *Buffalo Courier-Express* gave a prior discourse in his column, "As I See It," in the June 7, 1963, issue as follows: "Jeff Keenan of Portland, Oregon, is in town completing arrangements for a ceremony Saturday on the International Bridge. During the event, the span's engineer in 1870, Sir Casimir Stanislaus Gzowski, will be enshrined into the National Railroad Hall of Fame. Keenan, former Buffalonian, is board chairman of NARHFAM. Directors voted to honor Sir Casimir's memory after the Canadian Port Office memorialized the former Polish nobleman by issuing a postage stamp in commemoration of his 150th birthday last March.

"Philatelists as well as railroad 'buffs' requested 'Enshrinement Day' covers after this corner reported last February that Keenan was planning a Gzowski ceremony. To comply, he ordered a large supply of Gzowski postage stamps a month ago. And as soon as he arrived in Buffalo, the West Coast resident started looking for souvenir postcards bearing a photo of the bridge.

"Unfortunately, a thorough search of shops in Buffalo and Niagara Falls failed to turn up a single card with the International Bridge picture. It seems newer spans are commanding tourist interest these days. As a last resort, Keenan decided to try stationery and trinket stores in Fort Erie. In Bernie's on Jarvis Street, clerk Edel Jensen nodded affirmatively when he told her what he sought. Reaching under the counter, she removed a card, handed it to Keenan and said he could have all he wanted.

"Scarcely believing his good fortune, the customer said the sample was perfect and added, I'll take 300. Mrs. Jensen's eyes widened but she was able to make good her offer—with a few left over.

"According to Mrs. Bernie Morse, the 35-year-old cards were on hand when she and her husband bought the store in 1956. The owners hardly expected to sell a dozen in the next ten

90 years ago Sir Casimir Gzowski engineered construction of the great International Bridge across Niagara River linking Fort Erie with Buffalo. He also built the Great Western Railroad now part of Canadian National Railways.
As of March 5, 1963, the Canadian Post Office Department bestowed philatelic honors on Sir Casimir (see stamp affixed). 53 years ago C. J. (Jeff) Keenan as an engine foreman at the age of 18 piloted trains across the International Bridge.
On June 8, 1963, C. J. (Jeff) Keenan as Chairman of the National Railroad Hall of Fame presented the Certificate of Award enshrining Sir Casimir in the Hall of Fame to Mr. W. C. Bowra, General Manager, Great Lakes Region, Canadian National Railways, as the special train came to a stop at the bridge marker indicating the boundary line between Canada and United States.
This special event was a "First of its kind" in railroad annals.

At top is front view of Canadian postcard honoring Sir Casimir Gzowski, engineer for the International Railway Bridge at Fort Erie, Ontario, Canada. Below is the reverse of the card giving the history of this famous bridge. As an engineer and educator, Sir Casimir Stanislaus Gzowski took an active interest in Canada's development from the start until his death. He was the first chairman of the Commission for the establishment of Queen Victoria Niagara Falls Park (forerunner of the present Niagara Parks Commission), was made a Colonel and Aide-de-Camp to Queen Victoria in 1879, and was knighted in 1890.

years—to say nothing of disposing of almost the entire lot in one fell swoop. The special cacheted cover post card saluting Sir Casimir shows a picture of the International Bridge and was postmarked at Fort Erie, Ontario, on June 8, 1963, relating that 90 years ago Sir Casimir Gzowski engineered construction of the great International Bridge across the Niagara River linking Fort Erie with Buffalo. He also built the Great Western Railroad now part of the Canadian National Railways. As of March 5, 1963, the Canadian Post Office Department bestowed philatelic honors on Sir Casimir.

Fifty-three years ago Jeff Keenan as an engine foreman at the age of 18 piloted trains across the International Bridge. On June 8, 1963, Jeff Keenan as Chairman of the National Railroad Hall of Fame presented the Certificate of Award enshrining Sir Casimir in the Hall of Fame to Mr. W.C. Bowra, General Manager, Great Lakes Region, Canadian National Railways, as the special train came to a stop at the bridge marker indicating the boundary line between Canada and United States. This special event was a 'First of its kind' in railroad annals."

Golden Anniversary

BROADWAY LIMITED

The Pennsylvania Special, powered by number
1395, the high-mounted American Standard,
gathers speed on her maiden trip, June 15, 1902.
The Special was later re-named the Broadway
Limited.

Sponsored
by the
Casey Jones
Railroad
Unit

of the
American
Topical
Association

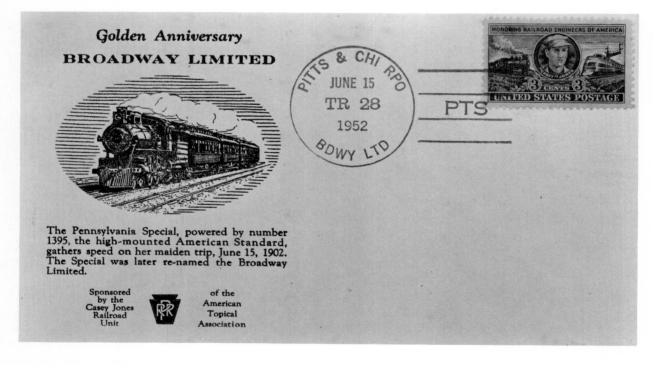

The Broadway Limited was a wonder in the railroad world—the peer in equipment, services, cuisine and operational technique of the New York Central's Twentieth Century
Limited. It glittered from locomotive pilot beam to the brass-railed platform of its observation lounge.

Commemorating The Inaugural
Run of The New Faster North

Coast Limited From Portland
to Chicago, November 16,'52

Commemorating The Inaugural
Run of The Mainstreeter

From Portland to Chicago
November 16, 1952

CHARLES J. KEENAN
6354 N.E. Cleveland Ave.
Portland 11, Oregon

Had not the Monad been adopted as the heraldic symbol of the Northern Pacific, an alternate might reasonably have been a fine bushy set of whiskers such as adorned many of the carrier's principles and patrons during the wars of the copper kings.

Golden Anniversary
20th CENTURY LIMITED

First Century! Pioneer train in 1902, powered by
Atlantic type number 2967, nearing Schenectady,
New York. ℗ New York Central & Hudson
River Railroad — The parent road of the New
York Central System.

Sponsored
by the
Casey Jones
Railroad
Unit

of the
American
Topical
Association

Golden Anniversary
20th CENTURY LIMITED

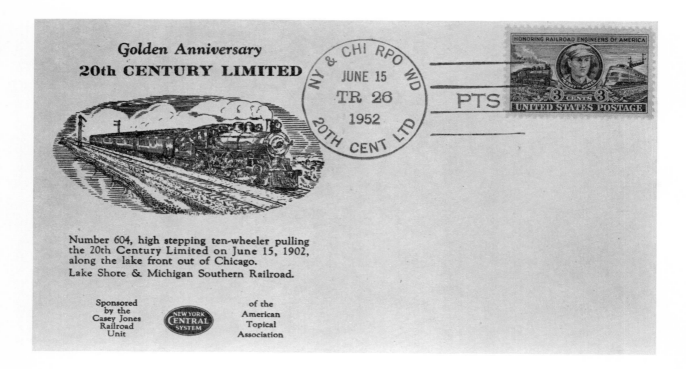

Number 604, high stepping ten-wheeler pulling
the 20th Century Limited on June 15, 1902,
along the lake front out of Chicago.
Lake Shore & Michigan Southern Railroad.

Sponsored
by the
Casey Jones
Railroad
Unit

of the
American
Topical
Association

A name train whose legend and excellences have exhausted the superlative, the New York
Central Twentieth Century Limited on the New York - Chicago run was, for decades on
end, the most celebrated train in the world. Placed in service in 1902, it became with time,
a national institution.

EMBAJADA DE MÉXICO

Washington, D. C.,
September 9, 1957.

No. 4561

Exp. 73-0/826.41/1

Mr. C. J. Keenan, Secretary
Casey Jones Railroad Unit,
6354 N. E. Cleveland Avenue,
Portland 11, Oregon.

Dear Mr. Keenan:

It gives me a genuine pleasure to confirm
officially to you the decision taken by the Government
of Mexico to issue a commemorative air mail stamp of
fifty cents (Mex. Cy.) value to mark the 50th anniversary of the death of Jesus Garcia in Nacozari.

The stamp's day of issue will be November 7
of this year. On this occasion I wish to tender to you
my congratulations, since this is the outcome of your
suggestion as per your letter of January 24, 1957.

With kind personal regards and best wishes
for your welfare, I am

Yours very sincerely,

Manuel Tello,
Ambassador.

Just prior to January 24, 1957, the author called on his Excellency, Manuel Tello, then Ambassador of the Mexican Republic at the embassy, Washington, D.C., suggesting that his government honor the memory of Jesus Garciz with a special issue of postage stamps on the 50th anniversary of Garcia's death. Garcia is considered the greatest railroad hero of all time, and this was the first instance of a government issuing a special postage stamp honoring a railroad personage at the suggestion of a citizen of another country. At top is first day of issue attached to postcard dated November 7, 1963.

Officials of the Spokane, Portland & Seattle Railway are as follows: left to right, H. W. Shield, general passenger agent; J. L. Monahan, assistant superintendent, operating department; J. C. Moore, traffic manager; also Ray Ryan, conductor, and Jeff Keenan, director of ceremonies. Ralph Wacther, locomotive engineer, is breaking the bottle of champagne over the pilot nose of the diesel locomotive. Until the year 1929, when the Empire Builder was placed in service in the Twin Cities—Portland and Seattle run—the Great Northern Railway's crack transcontinental had been the Oriental Limited. It was named for the Asiatic commerce which had been one of Jim Hill's objectives in building the railroad itself. The cacheted covers commemorate the new Mid Century Empire Builder and companion streamliner Western Star, on June 3, 1951, the latter taking the place of the Oriental Limited. Trainside ceremonies held at Seattle's King Street Station were represented by the Great Northern Railway.

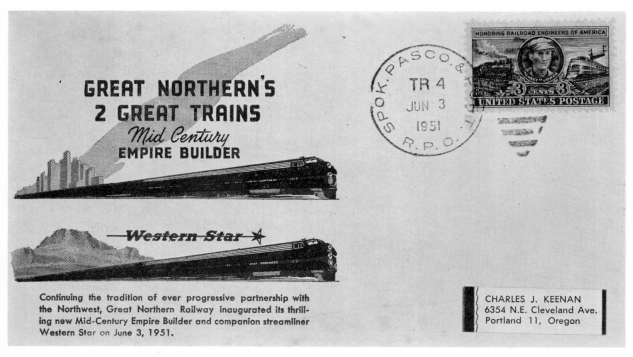

Postmark on cacheted cover indicates it was carried on S. P. & S. Train No. 4, from Portland to Spokane, June 3, 1951.

Trainside ceremonies held at Seattle's King Street Station were represented by officials of the Great Northern Railway as follows: left to right, I. E. Manion, general manager, Lines West; I. E. Clary, superintendent Cascade Division; A. H. Standrud, locomotive engineer, and Fred C. Gink, director of ceremonies.

GREAT NORTHERN'S 2 GREAT TRAINS
Mid Century
EMPIRE BUILDER

Western Star ✸

Continuing the tradition of ever progressive partnership with the Northwest, Great Northern Railway inaugurated its thrilling new Mid-Century Empire Builder and companion streamliner Western Star on June 3, 1951.

CHARLES J. KEENAN
6354 N.E. Cleveland Ave.
Portland 11, Oregon

Postmark on cacheted cover indicates it was carried on Great Northern Train No. 2, from Seattle east, June 3, 1951.

National Railroad Hall of Fame and Museum saluted the Tallulah Falls Railway for the important part played by Walt Disney's motion picture, "Great Locomotive Chase." Shown here is the cacheted cover issued at the Oregon Centennial Exposition and cancelled at the Centennial Branch, September 4, 1959.

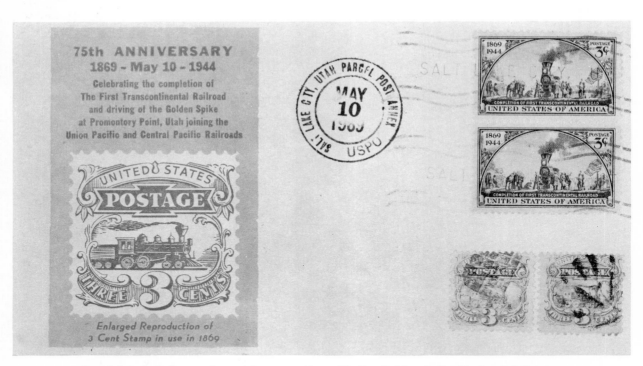

Special cacheted cover issued in connection with the Golden Spike Centennial Celebration. The lower commemorative stamps were issued in 1869, the initial date. The upper stamps were issued on the 75th anniversary, 1944, and postmarked May 10, 1969, the 100th anniversary, at Salt Lake City, Utah.

Philatelic honors were accorded to The Portland Zoo Railway on June 13, 1961, the first day of mail service. The Zoo Line was the first recreational railroad to carry U.S. Mail. All letters mailed on Zoo Line trains are postmarked Portland Zoo Railway, showing date of carriage, and they specify "Official U.S. Railway Mail—Mailed on Portland Zoo Railway— Portland Zoological Gardens, Portland, Oregon U.S.A."

LIVE STEAM. Joy of man and boy alike is the real, live steam engine. Zoo Line No. 1 was designed and built in Portland by "steam friends," George Burton, master mechanic, and his assistant, John Labbe, and others. It stole the show at Oregon's Centennial Exposition before being brought to the zoo.

NATIONAL RAILROAD HALL
OF FAME AND MUSEUM
C. J. KEENAN, Founder
Salutes
Association of American Railroads

the
most
important
wheel
in
America

JUNE 10, 1959
OREGON CENTENNIAL EXPOSITION
Portland Oregon

NATIONAL RAILROAD HALL
OF FAME AND MUSEUM
C. J. KEENAN, Founder
Salutes

JUNE 11, 1959
OREGON CENTENNIAL EXPOSITION
Portland Oregon

Philatelic honors were accorded for the first time to the Association of American Rail-roads, to The American Short Line Railroad Association, and to a different railroad each day during the hundred days from the opening day of June 10, 1959, to the closing day of September 17, 1959, of the Oregon Centennial Exposition. Cacheted covers issued by the National Railroad Hall of Fame were affixed with stamps commemorating the centennial of Oregon Statehood.

Walt Disney was in his glory during the little time he had to ride either side of one of his locomotives of the Santa Fe and Disneyland Railroad. The Fred Gurley was named after one of Santa Fe's former presidents. Shortly after his sixty-third birthday, a newspaperman who was interviewing Walt was struck by his frequent use of the phrase "It's fun" as he talked about his movies, studios, trains, Disneyland and his life in general. This led the author to ask, "What was the most rewarding thing in your life?" Walt replied, "The whole thing! The fact that I was able to build an organization and hold it. Some of the people at the studio have been with me for thirty-five years."

He was then asked to tell his greatest disappointment. "Nothing," he replied. "I used to kid my wife about not having a son, but now I have two good sons-in-law. Oh, I've had little disappointments, but I've gotten over them."

During "The Great Locomotive Chase"—Walt's cinema—he just couldn't keep away from the Yonah. He must have had an emotional interest in the little locomotive. If the Yonah had been disabled by the Andrew's raiders on April 12, 1862, to prevent further pursuit by Captain Fuller, the premise is that the raiders might have gained success.

PART THREE

GALLERY OF TRAINS AND LOCOMOTIVES

AMERICAN LOCOMOTIVES

Great innovations preceded by prophets. . .Oliver Evans, genius, born in 1775. . .demonstration in the John Stevens yard. . .Tom Thumb, first American-built locomotive. . .Stourbridge Lion. . .locomotives named like race horses.

Nearly all great innovations seemingly must be preceded by prophets, men for the most part ignored or ridiculed, who have the vision to comprehend the implications inherent in a new discovery or a new invention. Starting something novel, something that differs radically from what is currently believed, is dangerous. It used to be common practice to feed prophets a stout dose of hemlock brew, or simply burn them at the stake. In any period the role of prophet is no life of joy.

One, and perhaps the greatest, disregarded prophets of the steam railroad in the United States was a persistent and cantankerous genius born Oliver Evans in 1755, in Delaware. When he was seventeen he read about the steam engine that James Watt had recently perfected in England, and from that point to the end of his life Evans's great ambition was the utilization of the steam engine, chiefly as a locomotive.

Oliver Evans, in 1813, said: "I do verily believe that carriages propelled by steam will come into general use, and travel at the rate of 300 miles a day." In 1819, Evans died, still unshaken in his belief in steam engines hauling carriages on rails. But, he added wistfully, as he thought of the doggedness with which his fellows held to old ways, "one step in a generation is all we can hope for. If the present generation shall adopt canals, the next may try the railway with horses, and the third generation use the steam carriage."

The steam carriage would not have to wait so long. A few other fanatics had seen something of the same vision that had beckoned to Evans. One of these, John Stevens, was a fanatic of great energy and ability. A veteran of the Revolution, Stevens had been preaching railroads even in Evans's time. And in 1821, he got from New Jersey a charter to build a railroad across that state, and two years later another charter from Pennsylvania to build from Philadelphia to the Susquehanna River.

Close on the heels of the demonstration in Stevens's yard, the dam of ignorance and apathy that appears in retrospect to have been holding back the application of the idea of steam and rails seemed to burst. Maybe it was the snorting toy on the circular track at Hoboken. It was barely a year until the Baltimore and Ohio Railroad was chartered, and within twelve months more, actual construction of the line was under way, being touched off on a happy occasion, during which Charles Carroll, sole surviving signer of the Declaration of Independence, grunted slightly as he laid a stone to mark the spot where the first dirt was turned. But the B&O was not yet a steam railroad. Horses were its first motive power. When the Tom Thumb puffed successfully down the tracks in 1830, it became the first American-built locomotive to operate on an American railroad. It was constructed in 1829 by Peter Cooper, inventor and philanthropist.

The first locomotive that ran on rails on the American continent was the Stourbridge Lion, which was brought from England by the Delaware & Hudson Canal Company, and tried out near Honesdale, Pennsylvania, in 1829. The engine was selected by Horatio Allen, a pioneer engineer, who ran it in its American trials. It weighed seven tons and was reported to be too heavy for tracks and trestles: consequently, the engine was laid away and gradually dismantled.

In almost all the earlier locomotives the axles were held by the frames so that the former were

90

always parallel to each other. In going around curves, therefore, there was somewhat the same difficulty that there would be in turning a corner with an ordinary wagon if both of its axles were held parallel and the front one could not turn on the kingbolt. In 1831, Horatio Allen built the first locomotive with swiveling trucks. The principle was afterwards applied to railway cars and now all the rolling stock in America is constructed on this plan, which was first proposed by Horatio Allen in a report dated May 16, 1831, to the South Carolina Canal and Railroad Company.

Between 1803 and 1830, when the locomotive may be said to have become an established success, a number of famous locomotives were shown. They were named like race horses. Puffing Billy was built on the model of a grasshopper. The steel legs of the insect moved the wheels of the truck. Blucher, Hope, Black Diamond, Dilligence, Experiment, Royal Gorge, Novelty, and Sanspareil were well known. Rocket, built also by Stephenson, won over all competitors in a trial called the Rainhill contest in 1830.

The pride of our trail-blazing American ancestors was the early American locomotive. Brilliant colors and elaborate decorations were representative of the 1860's, particularly the ornamental metal scroll supports for the headlight and the bell, the bright brass boiler straps, and the profuse use of gilt trim. It was not uncommon to see a dozen different colors on a single locomotive—usually to suit the fancy of the engineer.

A locomotive is the central figure of a railroad. Some of the pictures of locomotives shown in this book are of those I have seen, or pictures of the same type. I have fired and/or run some of them.

Colonel John Stevens blazed the railroad trail in 1825 by designing, building and operating a small self-propelled steam engine. Circling a track on his Hoboken estate, it became one of the wonders of the New World.

The inventive genius of Peter Cooper was always at work, and in 1829 he built the "Tom Thumb" for the Baltimore and Ohio Railroad, the first successful locomotive to be used in America.

The first OLD IRONSIDES was accepted by the railroad, but its maiden unofficial run was disappointing to almost everybody. Two men alternately rode and pushed all the six miles to Germantown. The railroad operators were frankly dismayed at the performance, and were happy they still had their horses. The re-built Old Ironsides proved to be successful, and on November 24, 1832, puffed on to some point beyond Union Tavern, then returned to Philadelphia, a total distance of six miles.

BEST FRIEND OF CHARLESTON—The Charleston & Hamburg, on the advice of its chief engineer, Horatio Allen, had the first American-built steam locomotive built in New York, at the West Point Foundry. They quaintly named it Best Friend of Charleston, and in December of 1930, it pulled the first train of cars moved by steam power on track in the United States. The Charleston & Hamburg, six miles long, may be said to have been the first American railroad as the term is generally understood.

SANDUSKY—Built by Rogers in 1836 for the Mad River & Lake Erie, later to become part of the Big Four—Cleveland, Cincinnati, Chicago & St. Louis Ry. The Sandusky was the first to have a steam whistle, first to run in Ohio.

THE PIONEER—built in 1848—pulled the first train west from Chicago. It is on exhibit at the Museum of Science and Industry at Chicago.

THE GOVERNOR STANFORD—This one reposes in the Stanford University at Palo Alto, California.

TROY—Built for Rensselaer & Saratoga Rail Road Company, which started operation in April 1832. It was leased to the Delaware and Hudson Railroad Corporation, May 1, 1871.

THE HACKENSACK—A Rogers-built locomotive in 1860 for the Hackensack and New York Railroad, later to become a component of the New Jersey and New York, and then the Erie Lackawanna Railway.

THE TIGER—The Baldwin job that many people would like to have seen with the naked eye was The Tiger, one of a series of four engines built in 1856-57 for the Pennsylvania Railroad. Although the stack, firebox, and part of the steam dome are painted black, the rest of the engine exhausts the rainbow. Wheels and pilot are not only red but vermilion red. The boiler is a delicate rose, with the railroad's title done on a flowing ribbon and surrounded by curlicues in gold. The outside of the cab is gorgeous with scrollwork in gold, and underneath the window is a painting in natural colors showing a Bengal tiger obviously stalking some unseen prey in a jungle as green as emerald. The name plate, set well forward on the boiler, is in great Barnum-type letters, TIGER; another jungle painting appears on the side of the headlight; and to top everything off, an American flag flies from a special bronze socket atop the pilot.

THE CAMELBACK—Baltimore & Ohio No. 217. This famous model played an important part in the development of steam power. Designed by Ross Winans for B & O, locomotives of this type were constructed in the Mt. Clare Shops from 1846 to 1873, for use primarily in freight service. The name "Camelback" is derived from the fact that the extremely long firebox made it necessary to place the engineer's cab on top of the boiler. This humped appearance resulted in the Camelback nickname.

THE J. W. BOWKER—In 1873, Henry Yerington, general superintendent of the V&T, found occasion to purchase from the Baldwin works two switchers, one of which is the "J. W. Bowker," still preserved by the property of the Pacific Coast Chapter of the Railway and Locomotive Historical Society.

MINNETONKA—The name was probably taken from Lake Minnetonka, Minnesota. It was built in 1870 by Smith & Porter Locomotive Works of Pittsburgh, Pa.

FAST EXPRESS LOCOMOTIVE—No railroad was ever more a child of the state than the Illinois Central, and certainly no railroad ever did more for its parent than this one, nor with such speed. In six years the Central turned a lot of great open space into a busy and generally prosperous commonwealth—perhaps the most striking metamorphosis accomplished by a railroad anywhere. The Illinois Central was one of the first railroads to build a locomotive in its own shops—No. 137 under the direction of Samuel J. Hayes, Superintendent of Machinery, 1866.

THOMAS ROGERS—Though the early part of the 1840's was required to recover from the '37 panic, by the middle of the period the better-managed and financed railroads were making fair progress with expansion and also in improvement of rolling stock and operation in general. One striking advance was that made by Thomas Rogers of Patterson, New Jersey, who invented what he called counterbalancing. He put weights between spokes of the driving wheels of his locomotives, on the opposite side of the rim from the point where the driving and connecting rods were fastened to the crank pins. This simple procedure was found to make the engine ride wonderfully well and it also reduced the blow on the track occasioned by the revolution of unbalanced wheels.

C. P. HUNTINGTON—Central Pacific started service between Sacramento and Newcastle, California, in 1864, with Locomotive No. 1, The Governor Stanford. CP's third locomotive, the famous diamond-stacked C. P. Huntington, later became honorary No. 1 of the Southern Pacific Company.

No. 1—Built by the Cuyahoga Steam Furnace Company of Cleveland, Ohio, about 1855, for the Illinois Central Railroad.

HERO—Built by William Mason, in March of 1874—the first locomotive for the pattern to make Chicago the colossus of rails—grew out of two streaks of rust that had been the state-built Northern Cross Railroad, 50 miles of haywire between Meredosia and Springfield, Illinois. N. H. Ridgeley of Springfield, with his associates James Dunlap and Joel Mattison, paid $20,000 for this wreck, which had cost the State of Illinois $406,233. The new owners laid new rails, built a few bridges, purchased three locomotives and a few cars, then set up as a railroad. Things went well, so the road was continued on across the state to the Indiana border where it met the Lake Erie, Wabash & St. Louis, then building westward. A little later these roads were merged in the Wabash System, with a line into Chicago.

MISSISSIPPI—This was in the service of the Natchez & Hamburg Railroad before becoming a part of the Illinois Central System.

THE MEMNON—1848. It was nicknamed the "Old War Horse" because of its Civil War service in hauling supplies and soldiers.

LAKE SHORE & MICHIGAN SOUTHERN RY. NO. 1—Built about 1859 and known as a "William Mason" locomotive.

CYRUS K. HOLLIDAY locomotive No. 1 and two early passenger cars. (Courtesy of the Santa Fe Railway.)

Lake Shore & Michigan Southern Railway prior to December 31, 1914, before operations were identified with the New York Central Lines. This American-type 4-4-0 with the diamond was taken at the Elyria ore dock in 1889.

The old "Lake Shore" was noted for its small but resolute ten-wheelers. This one was passing through Ceylon, Ohio (1895).

THE BRECKENRIDGE—This one started operations June 16, 1873, and discontinued operations July 31, 1889. It was a subsidiary of the Colorado & Southern Railway Company. Most narrow-gauge railroads have been abandoned during the past seventy-five years.

Bluefield yard of the Norfolk and Western Railway in 1888, just a short distance from Abbs Valley, the center of a rich vein of Pocahontas coal, featured for its heating qualities.

Atlantic, Mississippi & Ohio Railroad No. 37. This picture was taken a few days before reorganization as Norfolk & Western.

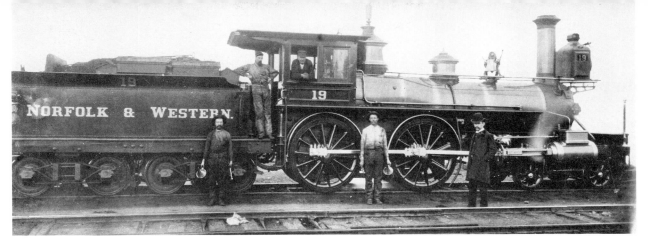

Norfolk & Western Railway locomotive No. 19 was of the same class as No. 18 used in work-train service by The Deepwater Railway out of Mullens. It was leased from the N. & W. because of the need of motive power.

Four TA class ten-wheelers were delivered from American Locomotive's plant at Richmond, Va., in June 1907. This class included Nos. 200, 201, 202 and 203, which were immediately leased by the N. & W. for passenger service during the Jamestown Tercentennial Exposition at Hampton Roads, Virginia, held in 1907.

N. & W. Railway passenger station and general office at Roanoke about 1902.

West Portal, Elkhorn Tunnel, West Va., N. & W. 1893.

Old Scioto Valley line train on ferry at Coal Grove, Ohio, N. & W. Ry.

Norfolk & Western No. 117, the first locomotive built in Roanoke shops, 1884.

Kanawha & West Virginia Railway locomotives Nos. 2 and 5 at Charleston, West Va.

Coal & Coke Railway No. 22, in passenger service between Charleston and Elkins, West Va., standing on a yard track at Elkins.

A WALTER McQUEEN—New York Central & Hudson River Railroad locomotive No. 862, an American type built by Walter McQueen, drawing the first run of the Empire State Express. The same train is portrayed on a 2-cent U.S. postage stamp issued to commemorate the Pan American Exposition, 1901.

It was the New York Central & Hudson River Railroad prior to January 1, 1915, when operations were identified with the New York Central Railroad Company. Shown here is the famous No. 999 of the Empire State Express, May 10, 1893.

Chicago, Burlington & Quincy (Burlington) No. 590—the Columbia type by the Baldwin Locomotive works just prior to 1899.

Freight yards and Union Depot, Portland, Oregon, prior to 1900.

Northern Pacific Terminal Company of Oregon, showing locomotive No. 1 in the vicinity of Union Station at Portland about 1907. Switchman at left wearing a derby hat was right in style on the job.

BIG FOUR NO. 6943, Atlantic type, shows C.C.C. & St.L—New York Central Lines. The author was sixteen years of age when he "fired" this locomotive, drawing trains Nos. 11 and 20, the Southwestern Limited between Columbus and Cincinnati, southbound, and a local, northbound, with Dale McCurdy as the engineer. No. 11 averaged eight Pullman cars and a baggage-buffet car with attendants who could mix drinks with adeptness for passengers aboard the train. No. 6943 was the author's favorite locomotive because "she" was a good steamer without having to shovel that extra ton of coal, which was the case with some locomotives, to keep up the 200-pound pressure in the boiler so important to the tractive effort of an Atlantic-type locomotive pulling eight to ten cars.

Coal was dumped into tenders just as it came from the mines. Sometimes it required getting back into the bunker with a coal pick to break up chunks weighing 50 pounds and more, that were blocking the path to he opening below the tail gates. Once it took the author several minutes to break up a large chunk, causing the steam pressure to fall back to 160 pounds, slowing down the speed of the train—and also slowing down the travel of the Royal Palm running from Detroit to Florida via Springfield and Cincinnati (near Franklin, Ohio), scheduled ten minutes behind the Southwestern. The photograph of No. 6943 was presented to the author by Tom Kennedy a few years ago. It was taken at the old Riverside (Cincinnati) roundhouse about 1916. The engineer, W. H. "Wild Bill" Hanrahan, and fireman Tom Kennedy were at that time the regular engine crew of the Ponce De Leon, a running mate of the Royal Palm.

P. F. W. & R. W., Pittsburgh, Fort Wayne & Chicago Railway, was operated by its own organization and that of the Cleveland and Pittsburgh Rail Road; later jointly with the Pennsylvania Company, and then with the Pennsylvania Railroad, now part of the Penn Central Company.

Wabash American-type locomotive No. 653, about 1900.

Illinois Central No. 201 served in interurban operation of the Chicago area. It was later retired to the Museum of Science and Industry at Chicago.

Norfolk and Western freight locomotive No. 475—class M. type 4-8-0.

Norfolk and Western freight locomotive No. 1238—class A, 2-6-6-4 articulated.

Norfolk and Western streamlined passenger locomotive No. 600—class J, 4-8-4.

Norfolk and Western coal-fired, steam-turbine, electric-drive locomotive No. 2300.

Virginian Railway locomotive No. 215, Train No. 3, at Princeton, West Va.

Virginian Railway articulated locomotive No. 700, XA 2-8-8-8-4, Baldwin of 1916. Dismantled in 1920 and rebuilt into AF 610 and 410.

Chicago Great Western locomotive most likely used to move equipment around repair shops. It is an unusual type.

Mt. Washington Railway—Hercules—a clog-gauge locomotive in service up Mt. Washington, New Hampshire.

Manitou & Pikes Peak Railway locomotive No. 3 is now retired and replaced by motorized units.

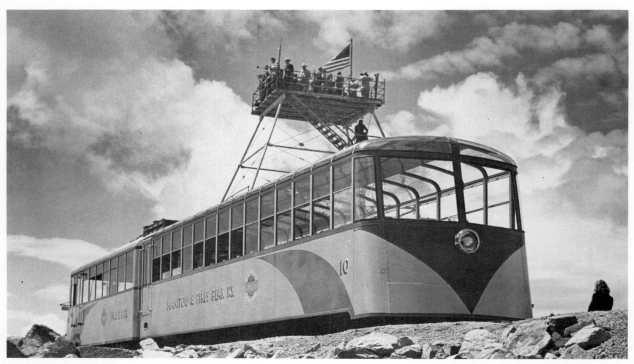

The cog train and the summit of Pikes Peak showing the observation tower from where an incomparable view of the surrounding region can be seen.

Mt. Beacon Incline Railway was one of the steepest of its kind in the world. Its two cable cars carried visitors to a lookout stop, Mt. Beacon, 1,540 feet above the Hudson River. This picture was taken in 1901, by the granddaughter of Colonel John Stevens. Another granddaughter is shown at right in picture. (Courtesy of Mrs. Frederick Trott, descendant of Colonel Stevens, who died January 10, 1972, at the age of ninety-three, in Ridgefield, New Jersey.)

Dr. Rudolf Diesel—The mystery surrounding the strange disappearance and death of the man who gave the world the diesel engine—forerunner of the diesel-electric locomotive —may never be solved. Rudolf Diesel was his name. In 1913, Dr. Diesel, then fifty-five and world famous, left Antwerp with two friends by channel steamer for England. In London, Dr. Diesel was to confer with certain business interests concerning the opening of a new Diesel plant. He and his friends had dinner on the boat and afterwards strolled on deck before retiring. Sometime during the night the famous inventor disappeared. Was he murdered? If so, by whom? And what was the motive? Or was it suicide?

More than sixty years have passed since that fateful September night in 1913, and the circumstances surrounding Dr. Diesel's disappearance from the *S.S. Dresden* remain as deep a mystery as ever. Whatever happened, it was a tragic end for the man whose invention led to the development of the Diesel-electric locomotive which now furnishes more than 90 percent of the motive power for the American railroads.

One of the first operations of the Union Traction Company of Indiana was between Anderson and Middletown, Indiana—later to be known as the Indiana Railroad.

Indiana Railroad chair car No. 54 in service of the Muncie Meteor.

BIG FOUR, Cleveland, Cincinnati, Chicago & St. Louis No. 396—first of the Atlantic type in service.

BIG FOUR Atlantic type No. 6951—one of the first locomotives to show the new corporate name "New York Central Lines." It also carries the same identification as before, "C. C. C. & St. L."

NEW YORK CENTRAL—In February of 1927, a new kind of locomotive was born, the Hudson type, designed for both power and speed on the water-level lines. The mastermind of this "Hudson" was Paul W. Kiefer, the system's chief engineer of motive power. Everything that the railroad had hoped for in its new locomotive design lived up to their expectations. The Hudson's performance became legendary and hundreds were ordered to speed passenger trains throughout the system. Shown here is Hudson type No. 5324, "King of the Rails." It was one of the greatest series of passenger locomotives ever built for the New York Central.

Hudson type No. 5363, about 1934, rolling down Main Street of Syracuse, New York. Later the railroad built around Syracuse, bypassing this route.

PENNSYLVANIA RAILROAD was highly successful with its well-known K-4s, a Pacific type that changed little over the years when competition kept bringing out larger and stronger power. Perhaps the success of the K-4s lay in their basically good design, right from the beginning, and standardization over the years. Two K-4s could haul 18 cars eastbound through Cresson, Pa., up the 1.5 percent grade at better than 50 miles per hour. Fortunately for esthetics, the K-4 kept going until the last. Those who have stood and watched a blue-ribbon New York-Chicago flyer whisk by at 75 miles per hour know the thrill that two locomotives chomping at the bit engendered. And those who were in the cab know how well a K-4 could perform. Shown here is No. 3655, a K-4 at Harrisburg about 1940.

Former Nickle Plate Road No. 759, a Berkshire, represents, perhaps, the ultimate in modern high-horsepower, high-speed reciprocating power as developed in the United States. She was built in August 1944. The 759 was completely overhauled in May 1958, but because of dieselization of the NKP, was never returned to service. For several years she was stored serviceable and later placed in the Steamtown Museum at Bellows Falls, Vermont.

It is with considerable pride that High Iron Company is now operating No. 759. After a stint of break-in runs, No. 759 drew the Palmerton Festival Limited on September 21, 1968; the Mohawk Valley Limited to Niagara Falls, October 12-13, 1968; two specials for the National Railway Historical Society out of Roanoke, Va., November 2-3, 1968; and the Golden Spike Centennial Train from points East to Kansas City, Missouri. No. 759 remained in Kansas City while the train continued on to Ogden, Utah. During her stay at the Norfolk & Western roundhouse, many persons, some of whom had never seen a steam locomotive, were in attendance.

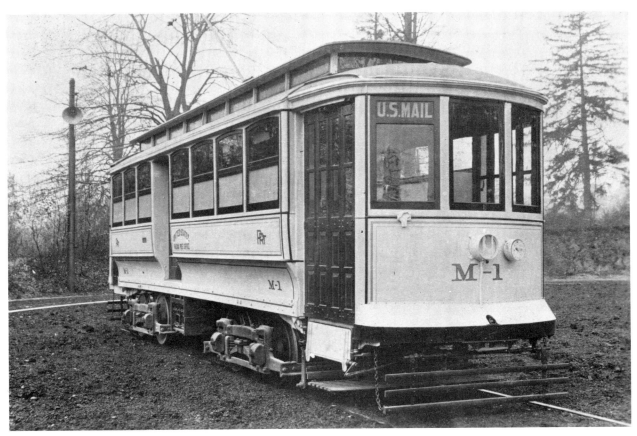

Philadelphia Rapid Transit Mail car No. M-1 carried U.S. mail for several years. This picture was taken in 1915.

Lower terminal near Government Camp.

Up 6,000 feet via Skiway to Timberline.

Timberline Lodge.

Tram returning to Skiway Terminal near Government Camp.

Skiway—Its first upbound and downward trips were made on February 3, 1951. This was the world's largest and longest passenger-carrying aerial tramway, providing comfortable year-round, tree-top-level travel above evergreens and crags for three scenic miles up the slopes of Oregon's majestic Mt. Hood. The tram was abandoned during 1957.

INCLINE RAILWAY—Operated by Porter-Carsten Log Company at Estacada, Oregon, this counterbalanced incline handled logs in connection with the Portland Railway, Light & Power Company, starting in 1923 and continuing for a few years afterward. It was hailed as the first instance in which an electric-operated railroad was used directly into the woods for a logging railroad. The incline was 2,800 feet long and had a maximum grade of 50 percent. (Courtesy of John Labbe)

Eastside Railway semi-open car, prior to February 5, 1901.

Eastside Railway "Inez" just after being raised from the Willamette River, where it ran through an open draw span of the old Madison Street bridge in 1893. Note the wheels on the left.

130

Portland Electric Power Company "juice jack" (got power from overhead wires) No. 1403, prior to August 29, 1946.

Oregon Water Power & Railway No. 101 in operation from December 6, 1901 to January 1907.

Portland Electric Power Co. middle-door car No. 1135—prior to August 29, 1946.

Passenger car No. 45 and officers' car, "Portland," of Oregon Water Power & Railway, in operation from December 6, 1901 to January 1, 1907.

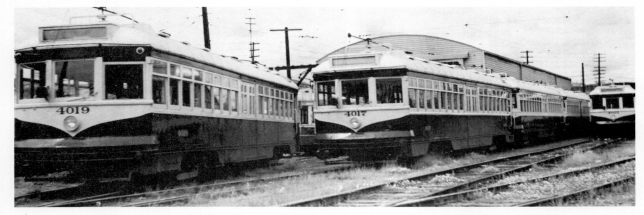

Portland Traction Company cars 4019 and others—formerly in operation in Los Angeles, California.

132

The Chicago and Indiana Coal Railway was a component of the C&EI. It was one of the few roads west of Buffalo, New York, that used camelback locomotives for motive power. This line ran between Brazil, Indiana, and Momence, Illinois.

St. Louis-San Francisco Railway (FRISCO) left its mark for a while on equipment employed by the C&EI. Extra freight, locomotive No. 1918, leaving Yard Center, a suburb of Chicago, on its way for Danville, Illinois.

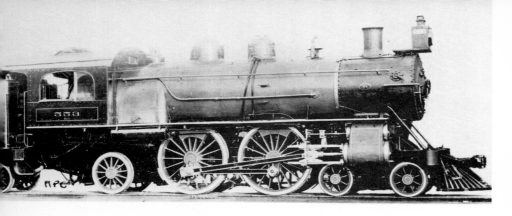

The 553 class could turn fast wheels to keep "The Dixie Trains" on time over C&EI rails.

The C&EI had a few bad wrecks One coal train developed a hot journal that was not discovered in time —resulting in cars piling up on both sides of the bridge at Milford, Illinois.

Train crews worked several days with the wrecking crews and their equipment to clear the tracks so the bridge builders could come in and build a brand new bridge. The author spent some time in the area.

The Beebe Syndicate consisted of 318 miles, Lockport to Syracuse and Oswego, New York, namely: Rochester, Syracuse & Eastern R.R.; Rochester, Lockport & Buffalo Corporation; Auburn & Syracuse R.R.; and other lines. The chair car, Palmyra No. 111, was named for the City of Palmyra, noted for its Mormon history.

Rooms over Pacific Electric Railway Hill Street station at Los Angeles were for years used as a club for P. E. Ry. employees. Card No. D-7133 issued to author's wife, Helen.

International Railway Pass issued to C. E. Denny, President of the Erie Railroad. International Ry. continued passenger service between North Tonawanda and Lockport after freight operations were returned to Erie R.R.

Jeff Keenan's Press card which served as identification for admittance to properties of the Stroud's Creek and Muddlety Railroad.

The celebrated Stroud's Creek and Muddlety Railroad wanders rather aimlessly through the ramp fields of West Virginia, its path much that of a happy child picking daisies. Those who care to pry know it is operated by the Baltimore & Ohio Railroad, which is an ordinary railroad. The SC&M departs from a B&O branch at Allingdale and goes westward for twenty-one miles and serves several coal mines. From Allingdale, a traveler on the SC&M—if travelers were carried, which they are not—might, by the way of Tioga, go to a point slightly beyond Muddlety. It may be worth noting that the SC&M runs very close to and seems to reach out in friendly fashion toward the Buffalo Creek & Gauley Railroad. Stroud's Creek & Muddlety! What better name for an amiable railroad running to a point slightly beyond Muddlety! After the B&O learned about its West Virginia operation with the enchanting name, its press agents lost little time. They began at once to issue press releases.

The press releases were written under a spectacular letterhead. It showed a mixed freight, drawn by an ancient locomotive. A banner, held in the eagle's beak and flowing back over its head, bore the name of the road. Underneath was the legend, "Linking Muddlety with the World." The press releases boggled the minds of stunned and unbelieving newspaper editors.

The Stroud's Creek and Muddlety Railroad began to link Muddlety with the world, or at least with the rest of the United States. Stories and editorials about the zany press releases appeared in newspapers as far away as Denver and Des Moines. Long before the fun began in 1904, the Stroud's Creek & Muddlety was established as an outgrowth of a lumbering operation. Whoever gave it its name is unknown, undoubtedly in honored glory.

Pacific Electric Railway—Railway Post Office Train No. 501, motor 1406 at San Bernardino yards, May 22, 1948.

Steam power was also used on Pacific Electric at that time. Here No. 1506 is switching cars at Watson, California, on the San Pedro line.

Excursion trains of the Vernonia, South Park & Sunset Steam Railroad operated between Banks and Vernonia, Oregon, over tracks of the Spokane, Portland & Seattle Railway. The first trip was on May 10, 1964, and the last trip on October 19, 1969. The operation was not discontinued for the lack of patronage but because of the great expense. This was a memorable scenic ride from the Tualatin Valley floor into the foothills of the Coast Range Mountains. The photo shows the excursion train crossing Mendenhall Trestle, one of the spectacular scenes along the route. This trestle was used as a setting in the filming of "The Emperor of The North" by 20th Century-Fox in what is described as a dramatic part of the picture. However, most of the cinemelodrama was filmed over the Oregon, Pacific & Eastern Railway in and out of Cottage Grove, Oregon. The railroad has been abandoned, but Oregon State Parks officials have plans to preserve the right-of-way for hikers, bikers and horsemen.

The 105, prairie type, has a historical record, unusual in various ways. It was built for the Oregon-American Lumber Company and later used by the Long-Bell Lumber Company at Vernonia. The photo, showing the author sitting on the left side of the cab, was taken by Harold Mehlig, a director of the V. S. P. & S. R.R., May 31, 1962. No. 105 is now on exhibit at Railroad Town, USA, Cottage Grove, Oregon

CANADIAN PACIFIC LINES
LOCOMOTIVES

Canadian Pacific Lines were noted for the building of fine steam locomotives at their Angus Shops, Montreal. The illustrations confirm the fact. At one time the CPR built some of their locomotives at the DeLorimier Works that was consolidated with the Angus Shops.

Esquimalt and Nanaimo Railway—the first train into the depot at Victoria, British Columbia, March 29, 1888.

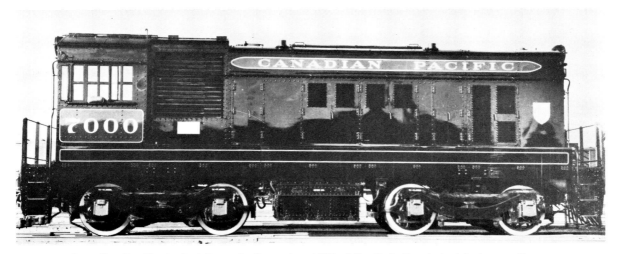

Canadian Pacific took delivery in December 1937 of its first diesel-electric locomotive, a switching unit numbered 7000.

Esquimalt and Nanaimo Railway-CPR diesel car at Niagara Canyon, a Victoria subdivision.

COUNTESS OF DUFFERIN—CPR No. 1. This was the first locomotive in Manitoba and on the prairies.

CPR No. 29, 4-4-0, built in 1887, was the last steam locomotive ever to pull a train on Canadian Pacific lines. It operated a special train from Montreal to St. Lin and return.

CPR No. 1066—When the author asked a switchman back in 1902 why a locomotive is referred to as "she," "He told me to be at the station when a CPR train would pull in and stop for custom inspection. I well remember it was a ten-wheeler. It could have been No. 1066. 'She' received plenty of tender, loving care."

CPR No. 1287—In the evolution of the steam locomotive, the 2-6-0 type represented one of the first trends away from the 4-4-0 type locomotive, the standard for freight and passenger service alike many years ago. The type name evolves from the fact that a number of units for China were among the earliest of their type built, the name honoring the Mogul emperors. CPR No. 1287 was one of the type introduced on Canadian Pacific lines in 1888.

CPR No. 1991—The "tank" type locomotive—so-called because it carried its fuel in a small bunker and its water supply in large tanks at the side of the boiler—is basically a European design. The Baltic Tank Type, 4-6-4T, CPR No. 1991, was designed especially for the Montreal Lakeside commuter service. Practically the same type was used in service of the Kanawha & Michigan Railway between Charleston and Gauley Bridge, West Virginia, transporting mostly coal miners from and to various points and the many coal mines.

CPR No. 2850—The efficient combination of high speed and adequate power characterized the CPR 2800 class 4-8-4 type engines. This type of locomotive was popularized by the New York Central Railway, which appended the class name "Hudson" to them, after the river which the NYC parallels between New York City and Albany.

CPR No. 3001—On test, September 18, 1936, a new lightweight, streamlined passenger train attained an official recorded speed of 112-1/2 miles per hour on the Winchester subdivision near St. Telesphore, Quebec, with a 4-4-4 locomotive No. 3003. This was the highest officially recorded train speed ever attained in Canada. CPR No. 3001 is of the same type. This, the Jubilee type, was similar to Santa Fe's No. 1010 that drew Scotty's Coyote special part of the way from Los Angeles to Chicago.

CPR No. 5018—The era of the fast freight train had come, and in spite of evolution toward a "super" locomotive which manifested itself in the 1920s and 1930s, the 2-8-2 remained the basic road freight locomotive to the end of the steam era. Their American type name, "Mikado," incidentally, was related to the fact that some 2-8-2s built for the Imperial Government Railways of Japan were said to be the first of their wheel arrangement ever outshopped. CPR No. 5018 was equally at home on passenger trains in hilly terrain.

CPR No. 5935—Measuring just short of one hundred feet long, the 5900 series of 2-10-4 type locomotives were the largest and heaviest steam locomotives in the Commonwealth. In the United States, locomotives of this wheel arrangement were known as "Texas" types, but in the 1930s, a competition conducted among Canadian Pacific employees resulted in the name of "Selkirk" being selected.

"Steamtrain"—National King of Hoboes

Seeing America on $0 a day—the hobo way—is a dying life-style, kept breathing by only a handful of rail-riding vagabonds. Gone, or almost gone, is the caricature of the classic hobo: unshaven face, ragged clothes, funny hat, stuffed kerchief on a stick across the shoulder, eating beans from a makeshift stove by the railroad tracks, sleeping in boxcars. That character belongs to the depression, but a few old-style hoboes, or reasonable facsimiles, still exist. One of the most articulate of America's compulsive hoboes is Steamtrain Maury Graham of Toledo, Ohio. According to Steamtrain's definition, a hobo rides trains. A tramp just tramps. A hitch-hiker is simply a hitch-hiker. A bum won't work, but a hobo will. Steamtrain informed me of his election as National King of Hoboes at their last convention held in Britt, Iowa, where their national conventions have been held since 1900.

In a recent letter from Steamtrain, he stated: "I just finished a complete circle of the U.S. visiting V.A. Hospitals. Each one was such a success, I just had to go on to the next. Somehow the men in hospitals just turned on when they heard there was a hobo in the hospital. Many would hold on to my hand and ask me to stay longer. It was very rewarding. I talked to some on their last day and others close to that day. They thanked me so much for coming to see them. I visited over 30,000 men, ending the tour at Cheyenne."

Steamtrain is a friend of Lee Marvin who played the part of a hobo in the cine-melodrama, "Emperor of the North," filmed in Oregon by 20th Century-Fox. Most of the action takes place along the Oregon, Pacific & Eastern Railway between Cottage Grove and Culp Creek. The most dramatic action was taken on a train moving over Mendenhall trestle near Buxton, on the Spokane, Portland & Seattle Railway, where Lee Marvin gave a realistic characterization as an "A No. 1" veteran hobo who accepts "Shack" (railroad brakeman) Ernest Borgnine's challenge to put him off while crossing the lofty trestle.

ACKNOWLEDGMENTS

Among the many people who have helped in the compilation of this book, I must cite Tommy Nichols, assistant superintendent, The Virginian and Norfolk & Western railroads, retired; United States Senator Stephen Benton Elkins, then vice president of the Coal and Coke Railway, Elkins, West Virginia; J.L. McKee, vice president, assistant to the president, New York Central System, Chicago, Illinois; A.S. Henry, superintendent, International Railway, Lockport, New York;

Colonel Elliott Springs, president, Lancaster and Chester Railway, also president of The Springs Cotton Mills, Lancaster, South Carolina; Robert J. Grant, assistant regional sales manager, and Charles Pribish, secretary to the vice president, Chicago and Eastern Illinois Railroad;

R.B. Kester, general solicitor, Union Pacific Railroad, Portland, Oregon; John W. Barriger, former president and "traveling freight agent," Missouri-Kansas-Texas (Katy Railroad), now special assistant to the Federal Railroad Administration, Washington, D.C.; Staff Officers of the Norfolk and Western Railway's Department of Public Relations and Advertising, Roanoke, Virginia; James Symes, president, Pennsylvania Railroad, retired;

Edison H. Thomas, manager, News Bureau, Louisville and Nashville Railroad, Louisville, Kentucky; J.G. Shea, vice president, public relations, Southern Pacific Lines, San Francisco; R.M. Van Sant, director of public relations, retired, and his assistant J. Carroll Bateman, Baltimore and Ohio Railroad, Baltimore, Maryland; Donald Gordon, president, Canadian National Railways, retired; and W.A. Johnson, president, Illinois Central Railroad, retired.

There are also a number of persons, in no way connected with railroads, who by their special knowledge were able to supply me with valuable information. Among them are William T. Bess, retired press correspondent; Lloyd D. Lewis and Bob Withers, staff writers, *The Herald-Dispatch*, Huntington, West Virginia; Colonel James G. Bogle, U.S. Army, retired, Atlanta, Georgia; Earl M. O'Connell, administrator - community relations, Westinghouse Air Brake Company, Wilmerding, Pennsylvania; and Honorable Frank G. Clement, in office at that time, as Governor of Tennessee.

I am truly grateful to Glenn O. Varnado, president, and William (Bill) Odbert, his assistant, of Kennell-Ellis, Portland, Oregon, noted for creative photography, and their staff, especially Mary Turple, who showed acumen and patience in the preparation of various items for illustration in this book.

Another to whom I am personally grateful is my loving daughter, Mrs. Mary Crum, who has been of immeasurable help during the production of this book.

Jeff Keenan

INDEX

A

"Abe Martin Line," 33
Aishton, R.W., 37
Albertson, L.W., 41
Allen, Horatio, 57, 91
American Locomotive Works, 29
American Railroad Association, 37
American Railroad System, 37
American Short Line Railroad Association, 78
American Topical Association, 77
Andrews, James J., 65
Andrews Raiders, 46, 65
Atlantic, Mississippi & Ohio Railroad, 58

B

Baker, George H., 41
Baldwin, 41
Baltimore & Ohio Railroad, 13, 14, 22, 45, 75, 90
Barriger, John W., 42
Bean, Ormond, 41
Bedwell, Harry, 38
Bellaire, Zanesville & Cincinnati, 14
"Bent, Zigzag & Crooked," 14
"Big 4," 29, 73
Bisop, Bill, 78
Black Rock Railway Station, 10
"Blizzard Mailman," 73
Booth, Ralph Harman, 9, 21
Bowra, W.C., 42
Broadway Limited, 76
Broady, Joe, 29
Brotherhood of Locomotive Engineers, 41
Buckley, Harry, 41
Buffalo Courier Express, 42, 78

C

Cacheted Covers:
  Baltimore & Ohio, 75
  "Blizzard Mailman," 73
  Broadway Limited, 76
  Casey Jones, 73, 77
  Mainstreeter, 76
  North Coast Limited, 76
  Shasta Daylight, 77
  Start of Railway Philately, 77
  Twentieth Century Limited, 76
"Camel-backs," 30
Canadian National Railways, 42, 61, 79

Canadian Pacific Railway, 58, 139
Canadian Post Office Department, 79
"Cannon Ball Express," 62
Cannon, Uncle Joe, 34
Carrol, Charles, 90
Charleston Depot, 18
Cheraw & Chester Railway, 45
Chesapeake & Ohio Railway, 22, 30, 58
Chessie System, 18
Chicago & Alton Railroad, 58
Chicago, Burlington & Quincy Railroad, 77
Chicago Daily Journal, 9, 21
Chicago, Milwaukee & St. Paul Railroad, 58
Chicago & Northwestern Rly. Atlantic Express, 65
Chicago Outer Belt, 34
Chicago Railroad Fair of 1948, 37
Chicago World's Fair of 1893, 76
Cincinnati & Muskingum Valley Railroad, 14
Clay Court House, W. Va., 18
Cleveland & Marietta Railway, 14
Coach of Fame, 38
Coal & Coke Railway, 17, 18, 21, 34
Coe, William Rogers, 58
Columbus Union Depot, 14
Consolidation of Railroads, 42
Cooper, Peter, 22, 57, 90
Cooper Union, 22
Corliss, Carlton, 37
Crocker, Charles, 58
Crocker, Dewey, 73, 77
Czolgosz, Leon, 10

D

D'Alesandro, Mayor Thomas (Baltimore), 75
Davis, Senator Henry Gassaway, 18
Dayton Union Station, 29
Deepwater Railway, 21, 22, 26
Delaware & Hudson Canal Company, 90
Detroit Tribune, 9
Disney, Walt, 45, 65
Dodge, Grenville Mellen, 57

E

Edison, Thomas Alva, 66
Elgin, Joliet & Eastern Railway, 34
Elkins, Kit, 18
Elkins, United States Senator Stephen Benton, 18
Elmira, Corning & Waverly Railway, 37

Empire State Express, 72
Enshrinements:
    Hall of Fame, 46 to 62
    Hall of Romance, 62 to 66
Erie-Lackawanna Railway, 33
Erie Railroad, 37
Evans, Oliver, 90
Everts, Jerry, 78

F

Fagan, Dick, 38
Fast-Flying Virginian, 22, 58
"Father of American Railroads," 46
Filson Club of Louisville, Kentucky, 61
Fink, Albert, 61
Fort Erie Depot, 42
Fuller, William A., 46, 65

G

Galway, Tom, 26
Garcia, Jesus, 42, 65
George, David Graves, 29
Ghost of Allatoona Gap, 46
Graham, Maury, "Steamtrain," 145
Grand Central Station, 77
Grand Trunk Herald, 66
Grayson, Mark (Buck), 41
Great Chinese Monad, 76
"Great Locomotive Chase," 45, 66
Great Western Railroad, 79
Gulf Mobile & Ohio Museum, 61
Gulf Mobile & Ohio Railroad, 73
Gzowski, Sir Casimir Stanislaus, 42, 61, 78

H

Hannibal & St. Joseph Railroad, 77
Harriman, Edward Henry, 61
Harriman Railroad Empire, 21
Hatfield Clan, 25
Hewitt, Abram S., 22
Hill, James Jerome, 57
Hocks, Bob, 41
Holbrook, Stewart Hall, 38
Holliday, Cyrus K., 57
Hood, General, 46
Hopkins, Mark, 58
Hubbard, Frank McKinney "Kim," 33
Huntington, Collis Potter, 58

I

Illinois Central System, 33, 58, 62
Indianapolis News, 33
Indianapolis Southern, 30
Indiana Union Traction Company, 33
International Bridge, 33
International Limited, 42

J

Jackson, Tennessee, Sun, 77
Jones, Casey, 38, 42, 62, 73, 77
Jones, Janie (Mrs. Casey), 62
Judah, Theodore Dehone, 57

K

Kanawha & Michigan Railroad, 17, 22
Kanawha & West Virginia Railroad, 17
Kimball, Frederick, 58
"Knickerbocker," 29

L

Lackawanna & Western Railroad, 33
Lake Erie & Western Railroad, 30
Lancaster & Chester Railroad, 45
Lehigh Valley Railroad, 30
Lincoln, Abraham, 46
Linn's Weekly Stamp News, 73
Locomotive Engineer, 41
Locomotives (American), 90
Locomotives (Canadian), 139

M

"Mainstreeter," 76
Mallet steam locomotives, 66
Mateos, President Adolpho, 65
Matoaka Gap, W. Va., 22, 25, 26
McConihay, Conductor Tom, 18, 21
McKeldin, Governor Theodore E., 75
McKinley, President William, 10
McMillan, Robert Taylor (Bob), 62
McQueen, Walter, 58
Michigan Central Railroad, 33
Mid-Century Empire Builder, 77
Missouri-Kansas-Texas (Katy Railroad), 42
Morgan, General John Hunt, 22
Morse Code, 17
"Mother Hubbards," 30
"Muncie Meteor," 33

N

Nacozari, Mexico, 65
Nacozari Railroad of Mexico, 42
NARHFAM, 37, 38, 78
National Railroad Hall of Fame, 21, 37
National Railway Historical Society, 38, 41
Nevins, Allan, 22
New York Central & Hudson River Railroad, 10
Norfolk & Western Railroad, 26, 29, 30, 58, 66
North Coast Limited, 76
Northern Pacific Railway, 76

O

Oaks Amusement Park, 38
O'Connor, U.S. Senator Herbert R., 75
Ohio River & Western Railroad, 14
Ohio State Museum, 65
"Old Rusty and Wobbly," 14
Oregon Centennial Exposition, 46
Oregon Journal, 38, 41
Oregon Trail, 75
Oregon Trunk Railway, 78
Oriental Limited, 77
"OS" of Trains, 17
Osborn, William Henry, 58

P

Pacific Electric Railway, 34, 37
Pan American Exposition, 72
Panic of 1857, 61
Pearson, Asst. Postmaster General Osborne A., 75
Penn Central, 14, 29
Pennsylvania Railroad, 14, 30, 38
Philately (Railway), 72
Pickens, "Fat" Tom, 14
Pittsburgh & Lake Erie Railroad, 42
Portland Traction Company, 38
Portland Union Station, 77
Portland Zoo Railway, 78
Post Office Department (U.S.), 72, 75
Postal Transportation Service, 77
Public Utilities Commission of Oregon, 46

Q

Quinlan, Bill, 29

R

Railway Philately, 72
Reames, C.W., 76
"Revenooers," 17
Richards, Rachel, 9
Richardson, Uncle Billy, 22, 58
Ritter Lumber Company, 25
Rockefeller, John D., 58
Rock Island Lines, 33
Rogers, Henry Huttleston, 21, 22, 58
Roosevelt, President Franklin, 74
Roosevelt, President Theodore, 34
Ryan, Neil C., 41

S

St. Louis-San Francisco Railway, 33, 42
St. Louis World's Fair, 29
Santa Fe & Disneyland Railroad, 66
Schrunk, Mayor Terry (Portland), 78
"Shasta Daylight," 77
Shelley, Katherine Carroll (Kate), 62
Sherman, General W.T., 46
"Skiway," 73
Smith, Sir Donald Alexander, 61
South Carolina Canal Railroad Company, 91
Southern Indiana Railroad, 30
Southern Pacific Lines, 37, 38, 42
Southern Railway, 29, 45
Spokane, Portland & Seattle No. 700, 38, 77, 78
Springmaid Line, 45
Springs, Col. Elliot White, 42
Springs, Colonel Leroy, 45
Springs Textile Organization, 42, 45
Stanford, Leland, 58, 61
Stevens, Colonel John, 46, 90
Stourbridge Lion, 90
Stroud's Creek & Muddlety Railroad, 136
Symes, James, 38

T

Tallulah Falls Railway, 46, 66
Teal, Mayor John M. (Fort Erie), 42
Tidewater Railway, 21
Tierney, Ambrose (Engineer), 21
Tigrett, Isaac Burton, 61
Timberline Lodge, 73
Toledo & Ohio Central Railway, 17, 18
"Tom Thumb," 22, 90
Trans-Missouri-Kansas Shippers Board, 42
20th Century Limited, 29, 76

U

"Uncle Joe's" (cigars), 34
Union News Company, 10
Union Pacific No. 3203, 38, 41
Union Pacific Railroad, 21, 38, 41

V

Van Horne, Sir William Cornelius, K.C.M.G.,
    58
Victoria Yard, 33
Virginian Railway, 21, 25, 58

W

Webb, Simeon T. (Sim), 62
Western & Atlantic Railroad, 46, 65

Western Union, 17
Western Star (streamliner), 77
Westinghouse, George, 57
White, Colonel R.B., 75
White, Helen (wife of author), 30, 33, 34
Wooten boiler, 30
"Wreck of Old 97," 29

Y

"Yonah," 65

Z

Zimmerman, A.F. (Al), 41